JOURNEYING WITH
BONHOEFFER

Six Steps on the Path of Discipleship

ANDREAS LOEWE and KATHERINE FIRTH

MORNING STAR PUBLISHING

Published by Morning Star Publishing
An imprint of Bible Society Australia
GPO Box 4161
Sydney NSW 2001
Australia

ISBN 9780647530627

Cataloguing-in-Publication entry is available from the National Library of Australia http:/catalogue.nla.gov.au/.

Scripture quotations are taken from the *New Revised Standard Version Bible*, Anglicised Edition, copyright © 1989 the Division of Christian Education of the National Council of the Churches of Christ in the United States of America. Used by permission. All rights reserved.

Original texts from Dietrich Bonhoeffer's *Widerstand und Ergebung* are taken from Dietrich Bonhoeffer Werke 8, copyright © 1998 Christian Kaiser Verlag, edited by Christian Gremmels, Eberhard Bethge, Renate Bethge and Ilse Tödt, *Widerstand und Ergebung: Briefe und Aufzeichnungen aus der Haft*, Dietrich Bonhoeffer Werke 8, Christian Kaiser Verlag, München, 1998 (Used by permission of Random House Group GmbH).

Quotations from Dietrich Bonhoeffer's *Cost of Discipleship* are taken from Dietrich Bonhoeffer Works 4, copyright © 1959 SCM Press and © 2001 Augsburg Fortress Press, edited in German by Martin Kuske and Ingrid Tödt, and edited in English by Geffrey D. Kelly and John D. Godsey, tr. by Barbara Green and Reinhard Kraus, Augsburg Fortress Press, Minneapolis, 2001. (Used by permission of Augsburg Fortress Press and SCM Press.)

Quotations from Dietrich Bonhoeffer's *Berlin: 1932-33* are taken from Dietrich Bonhoeffer Works 12, copyright © 2009 Augsburg Fortress Press, edited in German by Carsten Nicolaisen and Ernst-Albert Scharffenorth, and ed. in English by Larry L. Rasmussen, tr. by Isabel Best and David Higgins, Augsburg Fortress Press, Minneapolis, 2009. (Used by permission of Augsburg Fortress Press.)

Images used under Creative Commons Licence CC-BY-SA 3.0: Fig 1, Fig 2 Bundesarchiv Germany. Image used under Creative Commons Licence CC-2.0: Fig 8, Cristian Bortes. Images in the Public Domain: Figs 3, 4, 5, 6, 7.

This edition first published in 2019

Typesetting by Brian Coyne and John Healy

This book is dedicated to some of our heroes
in the faith.

To Liselotte Schmidt (1909-1998) for her role as a principled
matriarch in the faith during
the Second World War and beyond.

To Canon William Watkins (1936-2018) for his radical
hospitality to so many young people
and his life of unwavering moral conviction.

To Rev'd Len and Rev'd Dr Jill Firth for a childhood and
the shelf of stories that prepared us for a life of mission and
resistance.

Wehret den Anfängen – Beware the Beginning

Praise for the book

"The studies create a wonderful interplay between
Bonhoeffer and St Luke, drawing the reader into a profound
and challenging sense of what it means to follow Jesus. The
language has both beauty and simplicity, engaging the reader at
every point."

Revd Canon Prof Dorothy A. Lee FAHA, Trinity College, University of Divinity

"A powerful and moving meditation on the life and words of
Bonhoeffer, and on the Holy Scriptures on which he meditated,
which shaped his life and his death."

The Revd Canon Dr Peter Adam, OAM

Contents

List of Images

Image 1: Dietrich Bonhoeffer, August 1939, in Waszkowo (Waschke). Photograph: Bundesarchiv Germany.

Image 2: Bonhoeffer on a hike with his Berlin youth group. Photograph: Bundesarchiv Germany.

Image 3: Entries from the register to the Lehrter Straße prison, showing the entries for Klaus Bonhoeffer and Eberhard Bethge.

Image 4: Handwritten letter from Bonhoeffer to Eberhard Bethge with text of 'Wer bin ich?' ('Who am I?'), July 1944. Photograph: Staatsbibliothek zu Berlin, Germany.

Image 5: Destruction in a Berlin Street from aerial bombing. Photograph: Sergeant A. Wilkes, No. 5 British Army Film and Photographic Unit, 1945.

Image 6: Picture of Flossenbürg concentration camp, Bavaria, where Bonhoeffer was imprisoned and executed. Photograph: US Army 99th Infantry Division April 1945.

Image 7: Handwritten letter from Bonhoeffer to Maria von Wedemeyer with text of 'Von guten Mächten' ('By good forces'), 19 December 1944. Photograph: Houghton Library, Harvard University, USA.

Image 8: Martin Luther King, Oscar Romero and Dietrich Bonhoeffer, sculptures on the West Façade of Westminster Abbey, London UK. Photograph: Cristian Bortes.

List of Abbreviations

KY	Kentucky
MN	Minnesota
MO	Missouri
NY	New York
UK	United Kingdom
USA	United States of America
SS	*Schutzstaffel*, Nazi law enforcement agency
Gestapo	*Geheime Staatspolizei*, Secret State Police
Nazi	*Nationalsozialistische Deutsche Arbeiterpartei*, the National Socialist German Workers' Party

Acknowledgements

We would like to acknowledge the Wurundjeri people of the Kulin nations, on whose lands, never ceded, this book was written.

We would like to thank the congregation at St Paul's Cathedral, Melbourne, and St James' Institute, Sydney, for inviting us to present the first versions of what would become this book. In particular, we would like to thank the people who took the time to come and speak to both of us after our talks about how much Bonhoeffer meant in their own lives, and who encouraged us to take the material and make it a book.

The complete German edition of Bonhoeffer's works was a generous gift, given successively as the volumes became available through the 1990s and 2000s, by Dr Brigitte Löwe.

To the people who read the book in advance, particularly Canon Dr Ruth Redpath AO and Hannah Hornsby, your input has helped us improve the book enormously. We would like to thank Dr Kris Argall, Amanda McKenna and the staff at Morning Star Publishing and Bible Society Australia for making this idea a reality. Jessamy Gleeson, writing wrangler, as always helped keep the writing projects in line.

We thank Augsburg Fortress Press, SCM Press, Gütersloher Verlagshaus and the Random House Group for permission to quote from the works of Bonhoeffer.

Introduction from the authors

Suffering

Miraculous conversion. Your strong active hands
are bound. Powerless and lonely, you see the end
of your actions. Yes, you breathe out and, silently and
confidently, lay the rightness into a stronger hand, and are
satisfied.
Only for a moment do you touch the blessed freedom,
Then hand it over to God, so that He
may gloriously complete it.

> From: *Stations on the Way to Freedom* (August 1944)

Introduction

Dietrich Bonhoeffer is one of the leading theologians and martyrs of the twentieth century. In 2020, it will be the 75th anniversary of Bonhoeffer's martyrdom and the end of the Second World War.

Journeying with Bonhoeffer is designed as a six-week Lent or Bible study guide for small groups or individuals. The book introduces Dietrich Bonhoeffer's life and setting. It then has six studies: each chapter includes a reflection on a section of Bonhoeffer's 1937 book *The Cost of Discipleship* in the context of a Gospel reading, a newly translated poem or prayer from Bonhoeffer's time in Tegel Prison, and some discussion questions.

The book ends with a meditation on the way forward beyond this book, for those who want to incorporate the challenge of Bonhoeffer into their life, or to shape the life of their faith community.

The book draws on German and English sources, and draws clear parallels between the challenges facing Bonhoeffer in Nazi Germany, and Christians today in a time of increasing extremism.

In this series of reflections, we will be thinking about what it means to hear and respond to Jesus' call today. We will be looking at the demands made by Jesus on his followers – the things he tells us to do that are life-giving and life-lasting, and those things he tells us to give up and leave behind as we journey with him. We will be looking at how it is that Jesus calls women, men and children today – the ways in which we may come to know that we have been noticed by him, and been invited to come and follow him. And finally, we will be looking at what it means to know Jesus' call resonate in us in such a profound way that we may say that we belong to him so intimately as to be members of his body. We will do this by examining the good news of Jesus' life, death and resurrection, as recorded by St Luke, and by looking at the German theologian Dietrich Bonhoeffer's *The Cost of Discipleship*.

On 9 April 1945 Bonhoeffer was martyred in a Nazi concentration camp; punishment for his part in the conspiracies within the highest levels of German military intelligence to kill Adolf Hitler and overthrow his regime. He died in the final days of the Second World War. Just as the evangelists' story of Jesus can speak to us today with great immediacy, so Bonhoeffer's reflections on what it means to be a follower of Jesus can also speak to us as powerfully today as they did when he first composed them in 1938, the last year before the Second World War.

Dietrich Bonhoeffer's *The Cost of Discipleship* was written for a group of Protestant students and clergy who, like him, were opposed to the rule of fascism. From the outset of Hitler's coming to power in 1933, Bonhoeffer had seen the role of the church as leading a prophetic opposition to injustice. It was not good enough simply to take care of those who had fallen foul of the regime. It was the role of the church to stop the terror of fascism altogether. The church must not only 'bandage the victims under the wheel, but jam the spoke of the wheel altogether,' Bonhoeffer believed. His *Discipleship* was based on years of reflection and on a series of lectures delivered at his underground seminary in an abandoned school on an estate in Finkenwalde. The book developed his ideas about what discipleship meant and what it would require of people who followed Jesus.

In Lent 2019, the reflections were presented as a series of popular Lenten sermons at St Paul's Cathedral Melbourne, and the translations and biography were presented at a sold-out event at St James' Institute in Sydney. Many people came to these presentations specifically because Bonhoeffer had transformed their lives, particularly older members of the audiences. Younger people who learned about Bonhoeffer for the first time were inspired and excited to learn more. This book is suitable for small groups or individuals in both Protestant and Catholic parishes to undertake a sustained study of a hero of the faith.

How to use this book

Each chapter of the book is designed as a session: with a translated poem or prayer by Bonhoeffer, a paragraph from *The Cost of Discipleship*, a Bible reading put into context, extended reflections, some questions for discussion, and a prayer.

The six weeks of Lent would make an excellent period in which to read this book, either in a group or on your own—both because Lent is a time of repentance, preparation and study, but also because Bonhoeffer was martyred on 9 April 1945 and the anniversary will typically fall in the Lenten period. In fact, in 2020 it will be the 75th anniversary of Bonhoeffer's execution, and 9 April will be Maundy Thursday.

However, the book could be used at any other time during the year, as the message of Bonhoeffer's life and thought is relevant to our Christian journey when we are facing times of difficulty, when we are helping others, in times of political challenge, or when we are trying to live in community with our God and our fellow Christians—in short, at any time. Perhaps you could use this book in different ways at different times.

We have gained so much from going back multiple times to Bonhoeffer's words and life as we wrote this book. We hope you also have a chance to go deeper as you engage in different ways with the ideas presented here.

Using this book in groups

Bonhoeffer was willing to be flexible in order to build community and live as a disciple of Christ. He met people where they were. His brilliant students at the University of Berlin got challenging and intellectual lectures; but the children and teenagers in Harlem, Wedding and Sydenham (disadvantaged areas of New York, Berlin and London) got fun and engaging classes. He was willing to live in community with ordinands; but when the seminaries were shut down by the Gestapo, and when he was in prison, he was willing to write the prayers and teaching down and circulate them by letter. In public lectures like 'The Church and the Jewish Question' he was unafraid to be radically political in criticising the Nazis; but hours before he was taken to his final court martial, he gave an uplifting sermon to his fellow prisoners in the concentration camp. We hope that this book will be used in different ways to meet people where they are.

Bonhoeffer regularly taught confirmation classes, and then was the director of a seminary, so the book could be relevant for adult baptism or confirmation classes, for church leadership professional development, or for a pre-ordination or clergy retreat.

We wrote this book first of all for our own context at St Paul's Cathedral in Melbourne, where study groups meet weekly through Lent. But we believe this book would also work for long-running small groups, Bible study groups or youth groups who meet less frequently. It could also be effective for an intensive retreat, where each chapter is a morning or afternoon session. However you meet, each chapter is a self-contained study unit.

We recommend spending some time each session

familiarising yourself with Bonhoeffer's ideas from *The Cost of Discipleship*.

Some groups love to have lots of reading to do at home, and value coming to the group discussion fully prepared. These groups should plan for everyone to read the whole of each week's chapter, or even reading from *The Cost of Discipleship* itself, and then working through the questions when you come together.

If you have a group where people don't have the time or inclination to read such a lot of words, there can be a presentation from the leader or a group member. The presenter can use the Biography and Reflection to plan what to say, and how to answer questions that might arise in discussion. Once you meet, you might get people to read the poem and then the Bible reading. Some people find reading aloud is uncomfortable, or find it harder to listen, so you could all read together in silence. Don't forget that people who speak English as a second language often find poetry more accessible than longer sections of prose.

There are questions in each chapter that help you to reflect on the theme of each week. You can work through all the questions, giving each an equal amount of time, or you can pick one or two that you want to focus on more deeply.

At the end of the session, we recommend you close with prayer. You can read the prayer we have included aloud, or everyone can read the prayer in silence. Alternatively, you can close with your own prayers, knowing our prayer is joining in.

Between sessions, people might like to put the prayer in a prominent place—as a reminder on their calendar, or pasted up somewhere they will see it like a pinboard or fridge. Every day until you next meet, perhaps the members of the group would like to pray that prayer.

Using this book as an individual

As an individual reader, you have the greatest freedom in the way that you use the book. There is nothing to stop you just reading the poems all at once, or just praying the prayers.

Perhaps you pick one chapter, that seems very relevant to you right now, and sit with it for a few weeks or months, reading it over and reflecting on your own responses and your own calling. Perhaps you sit down and read the whole thing, end to end (it is quite a short book!).

The other way we see this book being of particular use to an individual is as an accessible study guide on Bonhoeffer's life, thought and writings on the cost of discipleship. If you are reflecting on your own call, or you are a church leader or teacher who needs to help others with discernment and growth in their Christian journey, then this book can help you think deeply, encouraged by one of the most inspiring leaders and sophisticated thinkers of the church in the twentieth century.

Using this book as a whole church community

The reflections started out as sermons, so you can also use the chapter structure to help shape your weekly sermon series, whether in Lent or leading up to any time of commitment to discipleship. You might use it in youth groups for older teenagers (16+) or your young adults' group, if they meet separately. The questions might make good jumping off points for your own reflections, as you prepare your Sunday address.

Most churches already read sections of the Bible aloud each week, and you might want to use the Bible readings from this book in that time. The weekly prayer can be used as a collect, or in your intercessions. Three of the translations are from prayers written by Bonhoeffer: 'Evening Prayer', 'Morning Prayer' and 'Prayer in a time of Hardship'. Some churches like to have a mixture of poems and music for reflection, so you could use the translated poems in your worship time.

However you use this book, we hope you find it as inspiring, challenging, heart-breaking and soul-uplifting as we did to write it.

Notes on: Introduction from the authors

Suffering: 'Leiden', *from:* 'Stationen auf dem Weg zur Freiheit', Bonhoeffer, *Widerstand und Ergebung*, p. 571.

Biography of Bonhoeffer

Dietrich Bonhoeffer, August 1939, in Waszkowo (Waschke). Photograph: Bundesarchiv Germany.

The last days

It was spring among the Fichtel mountains, in the dense forests and blue-grey granite quarries of that part of Bavaria that runs close to the Czech border. But in a narrow valley, rows of tin barracks encroached into the mountains. As other concentration camps were hurriedly closed at the forward march of foreign soldiers from the west and east, the main camp and sub-camps of Flossenbürg swelled with thousands of men and women from Germany, Poland, the Soviet Union. They travelled to the main camp by train and then marched the final kilometres to the walled camp, through the metal gates, past the inscription on the granite pillar that declared *Arbeit macht frei* (labour makes you free). By April 1945, there were more people than work to do, either in the quarries or the Messerschmidt factories. The camp had always been overcrowded, and the prisoners had always suffered from malnutrition, disease, and a lack of fresh water. Many died of starvation or untreated sickness. Others were executed, often in large numbers at a time, by shooting, lethal injection or hanging.

On Easter Day, Bonhoeffer had been in special (and comparatively comfortable) prison quarters in Buchenwald concentration camp near Weimar, hearing the Allied guns in the distance and waiting to be liberated. On the Tuesday, with other special prisoners, he was evacuated by truck west and south, to Weiden, and then incorrectly sent further south to Regensburg concentration camp. They then had to be brought back by bus towards Flossenbürg concentration camp. On 5 April, Hitler had personally demanded the liquidation of high-ranking political prisoners associated with the failed '20 July' assassination plot. The group of prisoners made it as far as the village of Schönberg on Friday afternoon, where they were kept in a quickly repurposed schoolhouse.

For three days, the special prisoners waited. But for now, the views were beautiful, there were some potatoes to eat, the sun was shining, and there was a delay as they waited for the SS lawyer and SS judge to make their way right across the country from Sachsenhausen concentration camp on the outskirts of Berlin where, unknown to Bonhoeffer, they had just sentenced his brother-in-law to death.

A week later, it was another Sunday, and one of the special prisoners asked the pastor in their group to lead a service. Bonhoeffer consulted with the group of men and women—which included Catholics and an atheist—and with their permission he gave his final ecumenical service. It was an unlikely collection of people. Admiral Wilhelm Canaris had been head of the *Abwehr*, the German military intelligence, for whom Bonhoeffer had worked as a double agent since the beginning of the war, along with other high-ranking members the 'Canaris Circle'. A monocled English spy based in the Netherlands, Sigismund Payne Best, had been kidnapped during talks with German double agents in what came to be known as the Venlo Incident. Wassily Kokorin was the nephew of the Soviet Foreign Minister, Molotov. SS Dr Rauscher had been responsible for human experiments on concentration camp prisoners, but after being exposed as a medical fraud and accused of murdering his lab assistant, was now a prisoner. Six of the men were to be tried and executed in Flossenbürg, some of the others would be taken on to Dachau concentration camp near Munich, some to be executed, and some to be held until the camp was liberated.

The service was simple. Bonhoeffer read the texts for the day, said the prayers and explained the meaning of the Bible verses. The Old Testament verse was from the prophecy of Isaiah: 'But he was pierced for our transgressions, he was crushed for our iniquities; the punishment that brought us peace was on him, and by his wounds we are healed' (Isa 53:5). At that moment, Bonhoeffer reflected on the way of sacrifice taken by the suffering servant, who Christians believe to be Jesus on the cross, and the everlasting hope of salvation that was brought through him.

That night, Canaris, Bonhoeffer and four of their fellow

conspirators were taken to a drum court-martial at Flossenbürg. The trial was set up hastily in a laundry, without witnesses. The men were condemned to death. The next morning, the men were stripped, walked the scaffold and hung.

The early days

The twins, Dietrich and Sabine Bonhoeffer, were born on 4 February 1906 in Breslau, Silesia. This city had previously been Polish, Bohemian, Hungarian, and Prussian. Today it is Polish again, and called Wrocław. At the turn of the twentieth century, it was part of a united Germany which had only been formed 35 years earlier. The twins already had five older siblings, and three years later the family would be complete with another sister. Their father, Karl Bonhoeffer, was a neurologist, director of the Breslau psychiatric hospital and an academic at Breslau University. Their mother, born Paula von Hase, was the granddaughter of the academic Protestant theologian Karl von Hase and daughter of an academic judge. Thus, Dietrich Bonhoeffer was born into a large, well-educated, and socially well-connected family. His relatives were scientists, artists, diplomats, lawyers, doctors and theologians.

Paula Bonhoeffer had trained as a teacher and had spent time at Herrnhut, the community central to the Moravian Brethren Church (*Herrnhuter Brüdergemeine*). She hired Käthe and Maria Horn, Moravian Brethren sisters, as nannies and governesses to her younger children, and the three educated the children at home until they were old enough to go to secondary school. Paula worshipped at home, too, and rarely attended church services until the Confessing Church was formed.

In 1912, Karl Bonhoeffer was appointed to Berlin University and the Charité, the university's teaching hospital. In 1913, Dietrich Bonhoeffer began his studies at the Friedrich Werder Grammar School. The next year, the outcome of the Great Powers' stockpiling of weapons exploded in the Balkans, and German Empire entered the European War in alliance with the

Austro-Hungarian Empire. The two eldest sons, Karl-Friedrich and Walter were called up to active duty in 1917. Less than three weeks after beginning active duty, Walter Bonhoeffer died of wounds. Immediately, Dietrich Bonhoeffer decided to become a pastor, though he would delay announcing it until after his confirmation.

Bonhoeffer the Student

In 1916, the family moved to the Grunewald area of Berlin. The Bonhoeffers moved in a close-knit social circle. Family friends made through school and confirmation classes would go on to become colleagues, family and co-conspirators. Hans von Dohnányi was a school friend of Klaus Bonhoeffer, who would marry Christel Bonhoeffer, and his sister Greta would marry Karl-Friedrich Bonhoeffer. Von Dohnányi's friend Gerhard Leibholz would marry Sabine Bonhoeffer. Emmi Delbrück was a family friend who would marry Klaus Bonhoeffer. Ursula Bonhoeffer would marry Rüdiger Schleicher and they would live in the house next door when the elder Bonhoeffers retired to the Charlottenburg area of Berlin. Dietrich and Klaus Bonhoeffer, Hans von Dohnányi, and Rüdiger Schleicher would all be executed for their work against the Nazi regime; along with Klaus' brother-in-law Justus Delbrück, and Paula Bonhoeffer's cousin Karl Paul von Hase.

At the age of 17, Bonhoeffer left home to study towards his first degree as well as the Civil Service Entrance exam (as in Prussia, and later in Nazi Germany, the state was responsible for qualifying pastors). He travelled over 500 kilometres to the south-west of Germany, to study at one of the oldest universities in the country, at the Protestant Faculty of Theology of the University of Tübingen. His father, two of his brothers, and his sister Christel had already studied at the University. His studies were challenged by the rampant inflation that had affected Germany since the war. As he wrote in his letters home, within a semester the cost of textbooks rose nearly 80% and the cost of his meals more than doubled. Bonhoeffer belonged to a fraternity along with Walter Dress, who would be a classmate later at the University of Berlin, and would eventually marry Bonhoeffer's youngest sister Susanne and become an active member of the Confessing Church.

At the end of the year in Tübingen, Bonhoeffer suffered a concussion in a skating accident and spent the summer travelling with his brother Klaus to recuperate. They visited Rome, Sicily, Tripoli and the Libyan desert, and then spent some months studying in Rome. The Bonhoeffers were globetrotters—and Dietrich had their taste for travel. In 1924, Dietrich Bonhoeffer returned to Berlin to continue his studies as changing universities mid-degree is common in Germany. In 1927 he graduated *summa cum laude* (with the highest distinction). Bonhoeffer's academic credentials were impeccable.

The purpose of all of his study was always ordination. However, first Bonhoeffer needed to turn 25 years old to be eligible. He worked as a volunteer assistant pastor in a church in Berlin, and as a volunteer teaching assistant at the University. In 1928-29, Bonhoeffer served the German Congregation in Barcelona, Spain. In 1930, Bonhoeffer travelled to the United States of America to study at Union Theological Seminary in New York. There he would be taught by Reinhold Niebuhr who became a life-long mentor. There too, Bonhoeffer came to be influenced by early Civil Rights movements through the African-American church. Frank Fisher, a black fellow-seminarian, introduced him to Adam Clayton Powell, Sr., under whose leadership the Abyssinian Baptist Church in Harlem had grown to be the largest Protestant congregation in the country with 10,000 members. Bonhoeffer helped to teach the Sunday school, and was inspired by the Gospel of Social Justice he heard taught there. In 1931, Bonhoeffer reached the age of 25, and so he returned to Berlin to be ordained.

Return to Berlin: 1931

Berlin in the 1930s was at the centre of a crumbling and disunited Germany. First World War reparations were crippling the economy, and the world was two years into the global Great Depression. Minor political parties were gaining influence. They were in and out of the courts and getting close to the necessary votes of no confidence to disrupt the German Parliament, the Reichstag. Protests, rallies and street fights led to violent clashes between gangs, political parties and individuals with guns, knives, clubs and firebombs. The Austrian banking industry had collapsed and inflation was even more out of control. But Berlin was also a centre for arts, literature, film and music, as well as for academic work.

Bonhoeffer was working as Lecturer in Systematic Theology at his *alma mater* when he was ordained into the Evangelical Church of the Old-Prussian Union, a church that had already had five names in the 60 years since the Lutheran and Reformed denominations were combined in Prussia to form the largest German Protestant Church. Alongside his mother's influence, this is another reason that Bonhoeffer's religious affiliations were more generically 'Protestant' than specifically Lutheran. One of the ways Bonhoeffer pursued ecumenism at that time was by working as Youth Secretary of the World Alliance for Promoting International Friendship through the Churches.

Bonhoeffer the anti-fascist

The leader of the largest of the extremist parties, the National Socialists, was made Chancellor in January 1933. Adolf Hitler, the Nazi Party, and its associated Brownshirts had been, for about 15 years, facing political and legal opposition for street violence, assassinations, political gun fights, and trials for high treason.

The majority of the German populace were what Hannah Arendt has called 'the slumbering majorities', who had been alienated both from governments made up of the social elite and technocrats, and from the violent infighting among extremists, and were no longer paying attention. They would be complicit in the Nazi regime across the next 12 years, either actively participating or 'just doing their jobs', 'just obeying orders'.

However, the Nazis were widely opposed by conservatives. This is why many of the names in the plots against Hitler are aristocrats or what John A. Moses calls the 'industrialist and commercial elites': military officers, and middle-class professionals. These were people like the Bonhoeffers, who valued the rule of law and the modern, educational and technological united Germany that had been created by Chancellor Otto von Bismarck and scientists like Alexander von Humboldt. Other opposition was raised by communists and socialists, by anarchists, by trade unionists, by Jewish groups, and by many others.

When the Nazi Party decreed that all German Protestant Churches were to be brought together in a pro-Nazi Protestant Reich Church in 1933, more than 7,000 pastors formed the Pastors' Emergency League (*Pfarrernotbund*) in protest. This group would go on to form the basis of the Confessing Church in 1934. Up to 800 pastors from the church would be arrested and jailed for their protests in 1937 alone. Others went into exile. According to Elizabeth Raum, about one third of pastors spoke out against the 'Aryan Paragraph' in 1933 (the requirement that members of all kinds of German organisations be of Aryan descent), though those numbers were reduced over the next decade as the persecution of outspoken pastors increased. It is likely that some of those who were not strong adherents of the 'German Christian' faction were undertaking quiet acts of resistance, though many were not.

It was impossible for objectors to remain within the new church after it had accepted the 'Aryan Paragraph'. The new leadership was so keen to strip the church of Jewish influence that it was proposed that the Old Testament be removed from the Bible. The first two times this recommendation was made there was such outcry that the proposal was forced to be rescinded. Yet in spite of the Reich Church's enthusiastic support of Hitler, soon it would be mandatory for all young people to belong to the Hitler Youth, which met on Sunday morning, and so the church was quickly made less relevant in society. Besides, the government found other ways to pursue their anti-Semitic agenda: from burning synagogues and books and destroying Jewish businesses on *Kristallnacht* in 1938; through tagging Jews with a yellow star from 1939; to the 'Final Solution' of total extermination from 1941. From the beginning, Bonhoeffer and his family could see where this was likely to lead, and in 1933 Bonhoeffer published a defence of German Jews in 'The Church and the Jewish Question'. Bonhoeffer's academic work and his freedoms were increasingly limited due to political interference from church and university leaders who opposed his inclusive views.

Bonhoeffer's colleagues encouraged him to leave Germany for his safety, and so he moved to London and spent some months as a pastor of two small German Lutheran churches, where he began work on the book that became *The Cost of Discipleship*. In the United Kingdom, Bonhoeffer built relationships with the Church of England, particularly with Bishop George Bell.

Bonhoeffer had been strongly interested in the Indian independence leader Mahatma Gandhi's ground-breaking work on non-violent resistance for many years. In 1935, Bonhoeffer received an invitation to visit Gandhi's ashram. Instead of going to India, however, Bonhoeffer heeded the rebuke of his mentor Karl Barth who reminded him that he was needed to resist the violent Nazi regime at home. There, he completed *The Cost of Discipleship*.

With the formation of the German Confessing Church—a non-legal church—had come the need for the education of new pastors outside of the traditional university structures. So it was that the Church set up five 'underground' seminaries. Bonhoeffer was the director of the seminaries in rural Pomerania. First they gathered in Zingst, up on the Baltic coast in the far north and then, when the unheated holiday cottages become unbearable with the onset of winter, 250 kilometres away in a former school at Finkenwalde in another part of Germany that is now Poland.

The small community was set up on the grounds of the von Blumenthal estate, neighbouring the grounds of the von Wedemeyer estate. It had been the work of Ruth von Kleist-Retzow (the grandmother of Maria von Wedemeyer, Bonhoeffer's future fiancée) to bring this together. Von Kleist-Retzow has been described by Jane Pejsa as a 'matriarch of conspiracy' for her role in bringing together conservative resistance to Hitler in the military and politics. As well as her work with the underground seminaries, her circle included Hans-Jürgen von Blumenthal and Ewald von Kleist-Schmenzin, local aristocrats and significant national figures who were executed after the failure of the '20 July' von Stauffenberg plot in 1944. Thus, we see that the women in this story are by no means fitting the Nazi slogan *Kinder, Küche, Kirche* ('children, kitchen, church') of the passive and private sphere—but rather they were active, powerful leaders and allies in the resistance.

The Seminary was declared illegal in 1936, and closed by the Gestapo in 1937, at which point it dispersed across the households of supporters like the Wedemeyers. Among the most important of Bonhoeffer's students was a mature-age student, Eberhard Bethge, who continued as the 'student inspector' working until 1940 with the scattered groups of ordinands attempting to continue their studies. Although Bonhoeffer was clearly a theological leader, he was surrounded by others who shared his commitment and who formed a community that strengthened and encouraged each other. Several members of Bonhoeffer's theological community were also martyred for their vigorous opposition to the Hitler regime.

During this time Bonhoeffer was also travelling to Denmark, Sweden and Switzerland, where he met with international allies. Karl Barth was forced to flee from Germany back to his native Switzerland. Bonhoeffer's colleague, Martin Niemöller, was arrested and sent to Sachsenhausen concentration camp, just north of Berlin; one of the camps with the infamous gates that declared *Arbeit macht frei,* also emblazoned on the gates of Flossenbürg, Auschwitz and Dachau. Bonhoeffer's university friend and Pastors' Emergency League colleague, Franz Hildebrandt, had to be helped to escape to England after being arrested. Bonhoeffer and Bethge helped drive Bonhoeffer's twin sister Sabine, his half-Jewish brother-in-law Gerhard Leibholz, and their two girls across the country, so that, like in *The Sound of Music,* they could walk into Switzerland and escape just as the authorities were about to close the borders. Confessing Church pastors were being arrested, interrogated, threatened, and their houses searched. Pastors were interned for short or long stays in the growing number of concentration camps for political opponents of the regime, the disabled, homosexuals, Jews and many others. There were physical fights in churches as Confessing pastors were wrestled away from their pulpits by Reich Church leaders.

Bonhoeffer the Double Agent

In 1939, war was declared, heralding eight months of waiting in the 'Phony War' (*Sitzkrieg*). Bonhoeffer was about to be conscripted; his lectureship was removed on recommendation of the Bishop for Foreign Affairs; and he was banned from speaking, writing or travelling without special permission from the Gestapo. So Bonhoeffer fled to New York in 1939. However, within days of arriving in the United States, he turned around to return to Germany, knowing that he was returning to eventual imprisonment and probably death. Bonhoeffer could have remained in America, avoiding conscription and working for international peace and understanding. However, once again he decided he needed to return to Germany and face the struggle there.

The resistance to National Socialism in Germany had not ceased. Bonhoeffer's brother-in-law, Hans von Dohnányi (pronounced now in the German, no longer the Hungarian way) had been part of the resistance since 1934. A lawyer with a doctorate in international shipping law and an international aviation law expert, he had been keeping a record of the Nazi's crimes so that when the regime fell, their leaders and members could be brought to justice. He had a senior role in the *Abwehr* (military counterintelligence) which surprisingly was, as F. Burton Nelson puts it, 'one of the primary centres of the resistance movement.' Under General Wilhelm Canaris the *Abwehr* is said to have enabled 500 Dutch Jews to escape to safety in 1941. Many Jews were given training as *Abwehr* agents and then sent abroad, where they were able to escape. Von Dohnányi would later be described by the Gestapo as the 'spiritual leader' of the multiple assassination attempts against Hitler that were supported or carried out by the *Abwehr*, as Elisabeth Sifton and Fritz Stern have described in detail.

Dohnányi recruited Bonhoeffer as an *Abwehr* agent, citing his international and ecumenical links as useful for spying purposes against the Allies. At the same time, his recruitment into the *Abwehr* placed Bonhoeffer in an excellent position to meet with Allies and their proxies in neutral territories like Denmark, Sweden and Switzerland as a double-agent.

The whole family was involved in, or supportive of, Dohnányi's and Bonhoeffer's resistance work, and actively opposed anti-Semitism. Raum describes how the family would meet at Karl and Paula Bonhoeffer's house, with a pillow over the telephone to avoid wiretaps, and the children sent to play outside to check no-one could overhear the discussions. The family developed codes to carry on their conversations. Eight members of the Bonhoeffer family would be arrested over the next six years, Bonhoeffer, his brother Klaus, his sister Christel von Dohnányi, his brother-in-law Hans von Dohnányi, his other brother-in-law Rüdiger Schleicher, Rüdiger's son-in-law Bethge (who had married Bonhoeffer's niece Renate in 1942), Klaus' brother-in-law Justus Delbrück, and their mother's cousin Karl Paul von Hase. Christel was released, Bethge liberated. The others were all executed.

The Bonhoeffers and the 'Canaris Group' collaborated with other resistance collectives, including the 'Kreisau Circle' with Helmuth von Moltke towards the successful Norwegian pastors' strike in 1942.

The 'Canaris Group' were also involved in multiple plots to assassinate Hitler, and in staging a coup which would enable them to stop the war. In 1943, for example, von Dohnányi helped smuggle a British-made bomb, disguised as two bottles of Cointreau, onto Hitler's plane. The bombs failed to go off. In January 1944, von Dohnányi and Ewald-Heinrich von Kleist-Schmenzin were involved in another attempt, thwarted because Hitler's schedule kept being changed at the last minute.

In early 1943, Bonhoeffer became engaged to Maria von Wedemeyer, a budding mathematician and granddaughter of Ruth von Kleist-Restow. Von Wedemeyer went on to be a ground-breaking female mathematician and computer programmer, and then manager in major US computer companies after the war, but she was only 18 at the time of their engagement. Only a few weeks later, Bonhoeffer was imprisoned.

Bonhoeffer in Prison

It was the currency violations, for sending money to the Jewish refugees in Switzerland that Dohnányi had helped save, that led to the arrests of Hans and Christel von Dohnányi and Dietrich Bonhoeffer in April 1943, along with other members of the *Abwehr*. Von Dohnányi and Bonhoeffer would never be released. They were kept in different prisons and faced repeated interrogation, illness, boredom, anxiety, and fear for their families.

Bonhoeffer wrote letters to his parents, to his student Eberhard Bethge who had since been conscripted into the army, and to his fiancée Maria von Wedemeyer. These are the letters collected in *Widerstand und Ergebung* (Resistance and Resignation), *Letters and Papers from Prison*, and *Love Letters from Cell 92*. Bonhoeffer and von Dohnányi were also passing secret coded messages.

Bonhoeffer's Three Prayers (see Chapters 1, 2 and 5) were written early in 1943 and are typical of his thinking and writing about his time in Tegel Prison—he reflects on his difficulties but also on his intentions. He wrote prayers, similar to the prayers he had written in Finkenwalde, carefully, using the Psalms as a model. In the prayers, Bonhoeffer expresses how he is prepared to suffer for his belief, and draws on his faith in God to support him, even as he fully recognises the horrors of his experience.

Of course, he was not writing without an audience. He was acutely aware of the need to encourage and reassure his readers (his parents, his very young fiancée, his student and now nephew-in-law Eberhard Bethge) that he was still alive, that they should continue to be brave.

For example, in 'Night-time Voices' he writes to Bethge:
Stretched out on my pallet-bed,
I stare at the grey wall.
Outside, a summer morning —
That is no longer anything to do with me —
is progressing, rejoicing into the countryside.
Brother, after this long night,
Our day will break.
We hold our ground.
Von Dohnányi took a different route. He was much sicker

and facing much more intense interrogation, and had many more people at risk if he slipped up or broke down and gave away any details. He asked his wife to bring food on one of her visits intentionally poisoned with diphtheria germs. There are some gruesome benefits in being the daughter of the one of the leading doctors of Berlin's university hospital. The plan was successful, and von Dohnányi was sent to hospital seriously ill. His interrogations by the SS and Gestapo were reduced until he was forcibly brought back to prison.

Bonhoeffer's poems were primarily written between June and September 1944. A final poem was written in November. There are comparatively few letters in this period, though Bonhoeffer continued to work on the draft of his theological books, and occasional authorised visits from his parents and fiancée continued until September. There were good reasons for this change.

In early June 1944, the D-Day landings had finally come, when Allied forces pushed into Normandy and began their final, successful liberation of the Continent of Europe from the west. Within the next weeks the '20 July' plot was due to take place: another aristocratic conspirator, Claus von Stauffenberg, would smuggle a bomb into Hitler's highly protected Military Headquarters on the Eastern Front, the Wolf's Lair. The bomb exploded and killed four of the people in the room, but not Hitler who was protected by a desk. In the aftermath of the failed plot, over 6,000 people were rounded up and most were executed: including Justus Delbrück, two of Delbrück's cousins, and Karl Paul von Hase, the City Commandant of Berlin who, according to Joachim Fest, was arrested while having dinner with the Nazi propaganda minister Joseph Goebbels.

The poems are a form of the coded speaking that Bonhoeffer had become used to. Back in the early 1930s, Bonhoeffer had learned to preach in a way that adhered closely to the Biblical message but that clearly held a political message of opposition for anyone who cared to listen. The family were all used to speaking in code during their regular meetings. The poems and prayers Bonhoeffer writes are both theological and political: they assure his readers of God's enduring care for him, but also his enduring loyalty to their cause; they await God's eternal hope, but also the end of National Socialism.

By this time, both Bonhoeffer and von Dohnányi were playing a waiting game, knowing that the Allied forces were coming ever closer. Von Dohnányi was in the sick bay of Sachsenhausen concentration camp on the northern outskirts of Berlin. He was alone, because Niemöller had already been transferred to Dachau concentration camp, just outside the Bavarian capital, Munich, three years before. Von Dohnányi was extremely ill with scarlet fever, phlebitis and diphtheria, paralysed in his feet and legs, and often left lying in his own filth for days at a time. Bonhoeffer remained in Tegel prison continuing to write, think, talk with his guards, smoke and wait.

On 22 September, however, the Gestapo investigating the '20 July' conspiracy found the documents documenting Nazi crimes that von Dohnányi had hidden. His role in the conspiracy was unmasked—he was in fact identified as the 'spiritual head' of the conspiracy, though he was not the most senior officer. On 8 October therefore, his close co-conspirator Bonhoeffer was moved to the prison underneath the Gestapo Headquarters in Prinz-Albrecht-Straße in central Berlin. He was almost certainly tortured and interrogated. Klaus Bonhoeffer was also arrested and certainly was tortured. Rüdiger Schleicher and Bethge, too, were arrested and held in jails across Berlin.

Bonhoeffer in the concentration camps

When Berlin's Gestapo building was destroyed in an air raid in February 1945, the prisoners, including Bonhoeffer, were moved to Buchenwald concentration camp near Weimar.

On 4 April, the diaries of the most senior officer of the *Abwehr* resistance, Wilhelm Canaris, were found. They were shown to Hitler, who ordered the immediate liquidation of the 'Canaris Group'. Von Dohnányi had been back in hospital, and his doctor, an anti-Nazi, heavily sedated him so he did not suffer as he was tried and hanged.

With the United States Army cannons close enough to hear, the other conspirators of the 'Canaris Group' were moved 250 kilometres to Flossenbürg concentration camp in Bavaria, at the southern end of the country and in the middle of nowhere. Their guards were under order to complete the liquidation, using whatever means necessary. This meant the judge who took the case was required to travel by freight train and then 20 kilometres by bicycle, for a night-time drum court martial. Before he was taken away to his trial, Bonhoeffer was asked to hold a Sunday service, where he preached on Isaiah, 'By his wounds we are healed' (Isaiah 53.5). In his last sermon, he used an Old Testament text, in an act of prophetic spirituality and political resistance. In this moment, Bonhoeffer clearly expected to take up his own cross—he was under no illusions about the horror, pain and degradation that were before him.

Canaris, Bonhoeffer and the others were hanged on 9 April.

The prison doctor later claimed that Bonhoeffer walked to the scaffold at peace and looking noble 'at the place of execution, he again said a short prayer and then climbed the few steps to the gallows, brave and composed. His death ensued after a few seconds'—a story that has been repeated many times, including in the *New King James Version Modern Life Study Bible*. However, the prison doctor's job was to revive people as they were being executed so that the punishment would last as long as possible, so his story is considered unreliable by modern historians. Other witnesses say the execution took six hours, which would be consistent with the usual practice. We can see why von Dohnányi's sedation was, in fact, a kindness. We know Canaris was stripped naked as a humiliation before being hanged and it is likely this was true for all the conspirators.

In short, Bonhoeffer's death was as horrific as he expected.

A week later, the camp was evacuated, and the prisoners were forced to march through heavy rain towards Dachau, thousands died on the way. Two weeks later, there were just over a thousand people left in Flossenbürg when it was liberated by United States Army soldiers.

There had been 85 raids on Berlin by Allied bombers in the previous year alone. Half of the city's houses were damaged and around a third uninhabitable. Estimates of the total number of dead in Berlin from air raids stand at about 20,000, with hundreds of thousands of people left homeless. On 16 April, the Soviet troops advancing from the east began the ground Battle of Berlin. On 21 April, they occupied the outer suburbs.

On 22 April, Klaus Bonhoeffer and Rüdiger Schleicher, were shot in the grounds of the Lehrter Straße prison where they were both being held.

Bethge's prison was liberated by the Soviet troops as the Red Army fought, and raped, their way through the city.

On 30 April, Hitler committed suicide. On 2 May, Nazi Germany accepted defeat, and the messy turn towards a post-war, Cold War, divided Germany began.

Bonhoeffer's Legacy

Eberhard Bethge had carefully saved all of his letters from Bonhoeffer, and it was his work that made the remarkable volumes of Collected Letters (including *Letters and Papers from Prison*) available. It is on these works, and Bethge's championship of them in Germany and internationally, that Bonhoeffer's position as a pre-eminent twentieth-century theologian and martyr is based.

In 2020, it will be 75 years since his execution. In recent years, historians have shown just how brutal Bonhoeffer's final months were, and how Bonhoeffer was part of an active family and large community of people working inside and outside of official structures to do the right thing. At the same time, popular culture has grown the myth of Bonhoeffer as an isolated individual standing up against an unstoppable regime, whose death was quick and composed, whose inspirational quotes (not all of which were actually ever said by Bonhoeffer) adorn posters and postcards.

We feel that the true story of Bonhoeffer's life and work is more powerful and inspiring, because it shows that we don't have to be a great leader or saint to be part of doing the right thing for each other in our communities and families. Bonhoeffer wrote *The Cost of Discipleship* for himself, as he made choices about whether to resist the National Socialist regime. But Bonhoeffer also wrote *The Cost of Discipleship* for his secret trainee pastors in the woods of Pomerania, who struggled with the choices of being arrested, being sent to the war zones where more than half of them would be killed, or swearing the oath of allegiance to Hitler.

Today, some Christians around the world face similar challenges. Where Christians are safe, it is our job to support our sisters and brothers who are being persecuted. It is also our job to make our communities welcoming to all people, regardless of race, ability, gender, health, legal status, or religion.

As Martin Niemöller famously said:
First they came for the communists, and I did not speak out—
Because I was not a communist.
Then they came for the trade unionists, and I did not speak out—
Because I was not a trade unionist.
Then they came for the Jews, and I did not speak out—
Because I was not a Jew.
Then they came for me—and there was no one left to speak for me.

Bonhoeffer did speak for all these groups, but yes, they came for him and the other pastors of the Confessing Church, and there was no freedom outside the prison walls either, for anyone to speak for him publicly, though we have seen many ways that people worked clandestinely to support him.

Germans have a well-known saying, '*Wehret den Anfängen*', translated as 'Beware the Beginnings.' It is often used to remind us not to wait until a disaster has unfolded, but to stay awake and aware of the early warning signs. Germany had 15 years of warnings before Hitler and the National Socialists gained power, and another decade before the 'Final Solution' was formally put into action. Bonhoeffer and his family and colleagues saw the signs, and stood up for what was right, starting at the beginning and staying true to the end. In our time and our place, we must do likewise.

Notes on: Biography of Bonhoeffer

Image Attribution: Waszkowo, Dietrich Bonhoeffer, August 1939 Bundesarchiv Bild 146-1987-074-16. CC-BY-SA 3.0.

The account of Bonhoeffer's last days is constructed from accounts in the following sources: Eberhard Bethge, *Dietrich Bonhoeffer: a biography*, Augsburg Fortress Press, Minneapolis, 2000; Sigismund Payne Best, *The Venlo Incident*, Reynal & Hitchcock, London, New York, 1950; Bonhoeffer-Initiative.com, https://www.bonhoeffer-initiative.com/en/#last-hours; Elizabeth Raum, *Dietrich Bonhoeffer: Called by God*, Continuum, London, 2003, p. 149; Nikolaus Wachsmann, *KL: A History of the Nazi Concentration Camps*, Macmillan, London, 2015.

The slumbering majorities: Hannah Arendt, *The Origins of Totalitarianism*, Harcourt, New York, 1976, p. 313.

Industrialist and commercial elites: John A. Moses, 'Bonhoeffer's Germany: the political context', in: John W. de Gruchy, *The Cambridge Companion to Bonhoeffer*, Cambridge University Press, Cambridge, 1999, p. 3.

The Church and the Jewish Question: Bonhoeffer, 'The Church and the Jewish Question', *Berlin 1932-33*, pp. 361-370.

Matriarch of conspiracy: Jane Pejsa, *Matriarch of Conspiracy: Ruth von*

Kleist, 1867-1945, Kenwood, Minneapolis, 1998.

Lectureship removed: *Illegale Theologenausbildung: Finkenwalde 1935-1937*, Dietrich Bonhoeffer Werke 14, edited by Otto Dudzus, Jürgen Henkys, Christian Kaiser Verlag, München, 1996, p. 126.

One of the primary centres of the resistance movement: Geffrey B. Kelly, F. Burton Nelson, *The Cost of Moral Leadership: The Spirituality of Dietrich Bonhoeffer*, Eerdmans, Grand Rapids, 2003, p. 28.

Spiritual leader: Elizabeth Sifton and Fritz Stern, *No Ordinary Men: Dietrich Bonhoeffer and Hans von Dohnányi – Resisters against Hitler in Church and State*, New York Review Books, New York, 2013, p. 126.

Widerstand und Ergebung: Dietrich Bonhoeffer, edited by Christian Gremmels, Eberhard Bethge, Renate Bethge and Ilse Tödt, *Widerstand und Ergebung: Briefe und Aufzeichnungen aus der Haft*, Dietrich Bonhoeffer Werke 8, Christian Kaiser Verlag, München, 1998.

Letters and Papers from Prison: Dietrich Bonhoeffer, edited by Eberhard Bethge, *Letters and Papers from Prison*, Schuster and Schuster, New York, 1992.

Love Letters from Cell 92: Dietrich Bonhoeffer and Maria von Wedemeyer, edited by Ruth Alice von Bismarck and Ulrich Kabitz, John Brownjohn, tr., *Love Letters from Cell 92: The Correspondence between Dietrich Bonhoeffer and Maria von Wedemeyer 1943-1945*, Harper Collins, New York, 1994.

Bonhoeffer's Three Prayers: 'Gebete für Gefangene', Bonhoeffer, *Widerstand und Ergebung*, pp. 204-210.

Night-time Voices: 'Nächtliche Stimmen', Bonhoeffer, *Widerstand und Ergebung*, p. 516.

Modern Life Study Bible: 'Dietrich Bonhoeffer: Radical Faith', in: *New King James Version: The Modern Life Study Bible – God's Word for our World*, Thomas Nelson, Nashville, 2014, p. 1415.

First they came for the communists: 'Was sagte Niemöller wirklich?', Martin-Niemöller-Stiftung.de, http://martin-niemoeller-stiftung.de/martin-niemoeller/als-sie-die-kommunisten-holten.

Chapter 1: Christ's insistent call

Bonhoeffer on a hike with his Berlin youth group.
Photograph: Bundesarchiv Germany.

Morning prayer (November 1943)

God, I cry to you in the early morning,
help me to pray and to gather my thoughts;
I cannot do it alone.
It is dark inside me, but with you is the light.
I am lonely, but you do not leave me.
I am timid, but with you is my help.
I am anxious, but with you is peace.
There is bitterness inside me, but with you is patience.
I do not understand your ways, but you know the right way for
me.
…
Lord Jesus Christ,
You were poor and miserable, caught and abandoned like me.
You know all the sorrows of humanity,
You stay with me, when nobody stays with me,
You don't forget me, and you search for me.
You want me to recognise you and turn to you.
Lord, I hear your call and follow.
Help me!

Bonhoeffer Reading: 'Follow me, walk behind me!'

What is said about the content of discipleship? Follow me, walk
behind me! That is all. Going after Jesus is something without
specific content. It is truly not a program for one's life which
would be sensible to implement. It is neither a goal nor an ideal to
be sought. It is not even a matter for which, according to human
inclination, it would be worth investing anything at all, much
less oneself. And what happens? Those called leave everything
they have, not in order to do something valuable. Instead, they
do it simply for the sake of the call itself, because otherwise
they could not walk behind Jesus. Nothing of importance is
attached to this action in itself. It remains something completely
insignificant, unworthy of notice. The bridges are torn down,

and the followers simply move ahead.

Discipleship, p. 58

Further reading: read the first half of Chapter 2 of Bonhoeffer's *Discipleship*, pp. 57-73.

Bible Readings:
Jesus calls the first disciples and a Rich Young Ruler

But when Simon Peter saw the catch of fish, he fell down at Jesus' knees, saying, 'Go away from me, Lord, for I am a sinful man!' [9] For he and all who were with him were amazed at the catch of fish that they had taken; [10] and so also were James and John, sons of Zebedee, who were partners with Simon. Then Jesus said to Simon, 'Do not be afraid; from now on you will be catching people.' [11] When they had brought their boats to shore, they left everything and followed him.

Luke 5:9-11

[27] Jesus went out and saw a tax collector named Levi, sitting at the tax booth; and he said to him, 'Follow me.' [28] And he got up, left everything, and followed him. [29] Then Levi gave a great banquet for him in his house; and there was a large crowd of tax collectors and others sitting at the table with them.

Luke 5:27-29

[18] A certain ruler asked Jesus, 'Good Teacher, what must I do to inherit eternal life?' [19] Jesus said to him, 'Why do you call me good? No one is good but God alone. [20] You know the commandments: "You shall not commit adultery; You shall not murder; You shall not steal; You shall not bear false witness; Honour your father and mother."' [21] He replied, 'I have kept all these since my youth.' [22] When Jesus heard this, he said to him, 'There is still one thing lacking. Sell all that you own and distribute the money to the poor, and you will have treasure in heaven; then come, follow me.' [23] But when he heard this, he became sad; for he was very rich.

Luke 18:18-23

The Bible Readings in Context

Jesus saw Levi sitting at his roadside collection point. Rather than pay the required toll, Jesus simply told the tax collector to come and follow him. And Levi got up, left behind his workplace and that day's takings, and followed Jesus. Later that day, he invited Jesus to his own home, and gave a banquet for the man who saw him, noticed him and called him to follow him. And he invited all his former colleagues to join in the feast.

In the Gospels, the call to follow Jesus is immediate and direct. Jesus comes to a workplace—the road toll station, the boat yard—sees and recognises those who are working there, and calls them to follow him. And the people whom he calls either leave all that they have behind and follow immediately, as in the case of Simon, Andrew, James and John and Levi, or they find reasons for themselves to reject that call and remain behind.

Levi turns his back on his old business. Indeed, he gathers his former associates around him in order to enable them also to experience the life-changing call of Christ. 'A call to discipleship immediately creates a new situation', Bonhoeffer explains: 'staying in the old situation and following Christ mutually exclude one another. The tax collector had to leave his booth, and Peter his nets, to follow Jesus.' We cannot both remain behind in our old lives and follow Jesus at the same time. We are called to leave behind all and to step into the unknown.

Those who follow, follow joyfully. They may leave behind their family and their livelihood, their business interests, but they follow with great expectation and joy. Some, like Levi, give a feast to celebrate their changed lives. Others, like the fishermen Simon and Andrew, put all they have in service of Jesus, turning their boats into floating pulpits, for example. Those who follow are changed, they let go of all they had in order to walk with Jesus.

There are also those who choose not to enter into discipleship, like the rich young ruler who approached Jesus in our third Bible passage (Lk 18:18-23). A man of substance, he had kept God's commandments all his life. But Jesus told him that, in order to follow him, he not only needed to obey God's commandments, but more importantly needed to let go of his possessions. That in order to follow Jesus, he needed to love Jesus more than wealth. Jesus, seeing the man, loved him, Mark tells us in his version of the story, and describes how the man wept as he walked away from Jesus' invitation (Mk 10:21-22).

The people who remain behind, are often deeply shaken by their decision not to follow Jesus' call. The rich man whom Jesus commanded to sell all his possessions, wept over his inability to give up and let go of his past life, and follow Jesus into an unknown future (Lk 18:22). His familiar circumstances would have remained the same; there would have been little change to the external rhythms of his life. Except for the fact that he had seen and been seen by Jesus, and heard and rejected his invitation to follow.

Bonhoeffer writes: 'Jesus only has one expectation of me, namely that I believe.' Like Levi, Peter, James and John, what do we need to do in order to follow Jesus readily and with joy?

Reflection: 'Walk with me'

'He got up, left everything and followed Jesus' (*Lk* 5:28).

In *The Cost of Discipleship*, Bonhoeffer showed how he understood Jesus' call to faith and service. Written in exile in London, under persecution in Berlin, and in community with the underground seminary at Finkenwalde, *Discipleship* was composed at a time when Bonhoeffer and his audience already knew what it could cost to follow Jesus. In this section of *Discipleship*—as in the lectures at Finkenwalde that were its first draft—Bonhoeffer reflects on Jesus' call to Levi, who responds by getting up and leaving everything.

Levi's ready response to follow Jesus is contrasted by the story of the rich young ruler. The young man lived his life in accordance with the ethical standards set by the Ten Commandments, but was unwilling to give up his wealth to follow Jesus. Bonhoeffer reflects extensively on this man's story: indeed, the young man's wealth may well have been a personal challenge for the comfortably well-off pastor. Bonhoeffer was used to ready financial support from his family, whether borrowing the family car and chauffeur to distribute Confessing Church materials, or being sent a grand piano so he could keep up his music in London.

Bonhoeffer, in examining what it means to follow Jesus faithfully, comes to the conclusion that the main concern 'is not that I have any worldly goods, but that I should possess goods as if I did not possess them, and inwardly be free of them.' What is important is not what I have, or don't have, but what I do. By all means have possessions, 'but have them as if you did not have them. Do not set your hearts on possessions.' Instead set your hearts on God. Indeed, Bonhoeffer believes: 'My faith, however, is not tied to poverty or wealth or some such thing. On the contrary, in faith I can be both—rich and poor.'

The realisation that setting our heart on God means changing other aspects of our lives will always be heart-wrenching. In the case of the rich young man, it was heart-breaking because his obedience was to his wealth, not God. Bonhoeffer writes: 'The young man is standing before Jesus, the Son of God. The full encounter is present. The only choices are yes or no, obedience or disobedience.' And grieving disobedience is still disobedience, is still not following. Dietrich Bonhoeffer says: 'First obey, do the external works, let go of what binds you, give up what is separating you from God's will. Do not say I do not have the faith for that. You will not have it … so long as you will not take that first step.'

The first people to be called into discipleship by Jesus realise that right here in front of them is God's living Word. God's own command made flesh is calling out to them to get up and follow.

Bonhoeffer explains: 'Here the gracious call of Jesus Christ to discipleship becomes a strict law: "Do this! Stop that!" Come out of the boat to Jesus', leave the toll booth and follow. And Levi, the toll collector, and the four fishermen hear and obey, and do what Jesus commands them to do: 'follow me', he calls, and they simply get up and follow. They hear the Word and do it without questioning whether or not they fully understand what is asked of them. Faith will grow out of that first 'doing', that first stepping out, Bonhoeffer tells: 'You believe—so take the first step! It leads to Jesus Christ. You do not believe—take the same step; it is commanded of you!'. This is a response made in faith, which enables faith to grow, and the actions of faith to flourish. It builds community and enables mutual growth and care.

'Faith no longer meant keeping quiet and waiting', Bonhoeffer writes, 'but going with Christ. Now all bridges had to be burned and the step taken to enter into endless insecurity, in order to know what Jesus demands and Jesus gives.' And just as each one of us has to discern how to follow the call of Christ, Bonhoeffer believed, so the church also has to discern what it means to go with Christ and speak out boldly in the face of injustice and oppression. Later in this series of reflections we will be looking again at what it means for the church as a whole to follow Jesus' call, what it may mean for us as a community to follow Christ. In this chapter, we will be concentrating on what it means for each one of us to step out in faith where Jesus leads.

For Dietrich Bonhoeffer, that stepping out in faith to follow where Christ led meant abandoning alternative careers in England and the United States and instead returning to Germany to step into leadership of the Confessing Church and membership of the Nazi resistance. For Levi in the Gospel stories, that stepping out in faith where Christ led meant abandoning his livelihood as a toll collector, and literally following Jesus. For both, the call to discipleship led to the acceptance of an unsettled, uncertain life. For us all, the call to follow Christ means to take the first step: to get up and start walking with Jesus.

Following Jesus means getting up and walking with Jesus, not sitting still. In the days before the call came, Bonhoeffer explained to his students, faith may well have meant staying put, doing good and waiting. 'But now Jesus was there; now his call came. Now faith no longer meant keeping quiet and waiting, but going in discipleship with him.' There is nothing wrong in principle with just getting on with things as they had been. But that's not discipleship.

If sitting still and just getting on with things as they are is not discipleship what, then, does discipleship look like? 'As long as Levi sits in the tax collector's booth and Peter at his nets, they would do their work honestly and loyally, they would have old or new knowledge about God', Bonhoeffer explains. 'But if they want to learn to believe in God, they have to follow the Son of God incarnate and walk with him.' And that is just as true today, as it was for Peter and Levi. We actually need to get up and walk with Jesus, in order to be his disciples. Bonhoeffer shows discipleship is not just having knowledge about God, but learning to believe in God.

Before we get up and act, we first need to listen. Listen to Jesus' words written in the Scriptures, and spoken to you by other followers of Jesus, the members of Christ's body. Attend worship in your community. You can listen to God by praying. Bonhoeffer taught that we should pray with thanksgiving, with petitions, but we should also sit in silent meditation with God. One of the best ways to hear Jesus' Word more clearly is to read the Scriptures. Joining a study group is one way to do that. Another way is to start a regular practice of reading the Bible on your own.

Be confident that Jesus will speak to you through the readings, the hymns, the sermon and our sharing in bread and wine. Be prepared to listen to what Jesus says. And then—and this, the story of the rich young ruler suggests, is the most difficult part of the process of discipleship—follow up on what Jesus says to you. This may well bring up areas in your life where you need to commit to change: this certainly is true for me, just as it was for Bonhoeffer who gave up his own material comfort and personal safety in service of the Confessing Church and the Resistance.

In the end, the only way in which we can become disciples is by hearing, and by believing in, Jesus' call. If the toll collector had had a conversation with Jesus and remained behind at his toll booth, he would have undoubtedly had better insights into his own life, Bonhoeffer warns: 'but he would not have recognised him as the one Lord, into whose hand he should entrust his whole life. He would not have learnt faith.'

By listening and acting, by following and accepting Christ's insistent call as true for him, Levi is given faith and a framework for life as a disciple. Starting to learn to have faith means starting to act on what Jesus calls you to do. Have faith to heed that call, and take the first step into discipleship by committing to walk with Jesus. Bonhoeffer put it like this: 'The first step is crucial. It is qualitatively different from all others that follow. The first step of obedience has to lead Peter away from his nets and out of the boat.' The first step leads Levi away from the toll booth and his past life. The first step leads us away from our preoccupation with our own lives to life with Jesus.

Jesus' disciples follow him simply for the sake of the call itself, because otherwise they could not walk behind Jesus. Jesus still calls each person to listen, follow and walk with him. And I pray that we might hear him call us and that he would help us follow him.

Questions: Christ's Insistent Call

When we listen to Jesus' Word, we can hear his will. And when we act on what he wills for us, we may learn to believe. And when we believe, we may step out in faith, ready to follow where he tells us to go. This call is extended to us today.

'What is said about the content of discipleship? Follow me, walk behind me! That is all', Bonhoeffer encourages us. 'Those called, leave everything they have.'

1. In Bonhoeffer's 'Morning Prayer', he says: 'I cannot do it alone', 'Lord, I hear your call and follow. Help me!' How could God help you to follow him?

2. In the Bible reading, Levi 'got up, left everything, and followed him.' What is the thing you find hardest to leave behind when you think about following Jesus?

3. Bonhoeffer says going after Jesus 'is something without specific content.' Does following just to follow Jesus feel scary or liberating to you? Why?

4. In order to hear Christ's call, we need to hear Jesus' word. Do you need to spend more time listening, rather than talking to God?

5. Bonhoeffer reflects that dispositions and life circumstances should be irrelevant in the face of faith: 'My faith, however, is not tied to poverty or wealth or some such thing. On the contrary, in faith I can be both—rich and poor.' Is there a 'some such thing' that you, or your community, thinks make it impossible for a person to truly have faith?

Prayer: 'Open my ears to hear your Word'

Lord Jesus Christ,
Open my ears to hear your Word;
Grant me the faith to know your will.

Open my heart to obey your call;
Grant me the grace to use your gifts.

Open my eyes to see the way you set before me;
Grant me your presence as I walk with you.

For in your Word I find my life,
and in your will my freedom.
In your ways I find my peace,
and in your presence my joy.
Amen.

Notes on: Christ's insistent call

Image Attribution: Dietrich Bonhoeffer mit Schülern, Bundesarchiv Bild 183-R0211-316. CC-BY-SA 3.0.

Morning Prayer: 'Morgengebet', Bonhoeffer, *Widerstand und Ergebung*, p. 204-205.

A call to discipleship immediately creates a new situation: Bonhoeffer, *Discipleship*, p. 62.

The young man asked about the path to eternal life *Discipleship*, p.73.

Jesus only has one expectation of me, namely that I believe: *Discipleship*, p. 76.

Not that I have any worldly goods: *Discipleship*, p. 78.

Have them [possessions] as if you did not have them: *Discipleship*, p. 78.

My faith, however, is not tied to poverty or wealth or some such thing: *Discipleship*, p. 78.

The young man is standing before Jesus, the Son of God: *Discipleship*, p. 77.

First obey, do the external works, let go of what binds you: *Discipleship*,

p. 66

Here the gracious call of Jesus Christ to discipleship becomes a strict law: *Discipleship*, p. 66.

You believe—so take the first step! It leads to Jesus Christ: *Discipleship*, p. 66.

Faith no longer meant keeping quiet and waiting: Bonhoeffer, *Discipleship*, p. 63.

But now Jesus was there; now his call came: *Discipleship*, p. 62.

Christ's call to discipleship dissolves all ties: *Discipleship*, p. 62.

As long as Levi sits in the tax collector's booth and Peter at his nets: *Discipleship*, p. 62.

But he would not have recognised him as the one Lord: *Discipleship*, p. 62

The first step is crucial: *Discipleship*, p. 64.

Morning Prayer: 'Morgengebet', Bonhoeffer, *Widerstand und Ergebung*, p. 204-205.

Something without specific content: Bonhoeffer, *Discipleship*, p. 58.

My faith, however, is not tied to poverty or wealth or some such thing: *Discipleship*, p. 78.

Chapter 2: Following Christ's call

Entries from the register to the Lehrter Straße prison, showing the entries for Klaus Bonhoeffer and Eberhard Bethge.

Prayer in a time of hardship (November 1943)

Lord God, great misery has overcome me,
My sorrows will overwhelm me.
I do not know if I am in or yet out.
God, be gracious and help me,
Give me strength to bear what you send.
Let fear not rule over me.
May you trouble yourself, like a father, to care for all of mine,
especially the women and children.
Protect me with your mighty hand
from all evils and all danger.
Forgive me all my sins
against you and against people.
I trust your grace
and give my life wholly into your hand;
Do with me
what you want and what is good for me.
I am at home in you, and you are at home with me, my God.
Lord I wait for your hallowing and your kingdom.
Amen.

Bonhoeffer Reading:
'I must be a neighbour to the other person'

Being a neighbour is not a qualification of someone else; it is their claim on me, nothing else. At every moment, in every situation I am the one required to act, to be obedient. There is literally no time left to ask about someone else's qualification. I must act and must obey; I must be a neighbour to the other person. If you anxiously ask again whether or not I should know and consider ahead of time how to act, there is only the advice that I cannot know or think about it except by already acting, by already knowing myself to be challenged to act. I can only learn what obedience is by obeying, not by asking questions. I can recognize truth only by obeying. Jesus' call to the simplicity

51

of obedience pulls us out of the dichotomy of conscience and sin. The rich young man was called by Jesus into the grace of discipleship, but the tempting scribe is shoved back to the commandment.

Discipleship, p. 76

Further reading: read the final part of Chapter 2 of Bonhoeffer's *Discipleship*, pp. 74-76.

Bible Reading: 'The Good Samaritan'

[25] Just then a lawyer stood up to test Jesus. 'Teacher,' he said, 'what must I do to inherit eternal life?' [26] He said to him, 'What is written in the law? What do you read there? [27] He answered, 'You shall love the Lord your God with all your heart, and with all your soul, and with all your strength, and with all your mind; and your neighbour as yourself.' [28] And he said to him, 'You have given the right answer; do this, and you will live.' [29]But wanting to justify himself, he asked Jesus, 'And who is my neighbour?' [30]Jesus replied, 'A man was going down from Jerusalem to Jericho, and fell into the hands of robbers, who stripped him, beat him, and went away, leaving him half dead. [31] Now by chance a priest was going down that road; and when he saw him, he passed by on the other side. [32] So likewise a Levite, when he came to the place and saw him, passed by on the other side. [33] But a Samaritan while travelling came near him; and when he saw him, he was moved with pity. [34] He went to him and bandaged his wounds, having poured oil and wine on them. Then he put him on his own animal, brought him to an inn, and took care of him. [35] The next day he took out two denarii, gave them to the innkeeper, and said, "Take care of him; and when I come back, I will repay you whatever more you spend." [36] Which of these three, do you think, was a neighbour to the man who fell into the hands of the robbers?' [37] He said, 'The one who showed him mercy.' Jesus said to him, 'Go and do likewise.'

Luke 10:25-37

The Bible Reading in Context

In the last chapter, we saw two possible responses to Jesus' call: immediately getting up to follow, or finding the call too costly and walking away. Of course, we may want to be more reasonable and ask questions before committing to following Jesus, but there is a cost to this too, Bonhoeffer says.

Jesus tells the lawyer – whom Bonhoeffer calls 'the tempting scribe' – in this parable that it is in doing the things that God commands that he will inherit life. When we do what God wishes us to do, we tap into the life that lasts. Because when we align our wills with his will, when we set our hearts on what he loves, then we already share in a life that is forever. Conversely if, like the lawyer in the Gospel story, we seek to qualify, to find reasons for why we may not be able to align our wills with God's, then we lose out, and do not find the capacity to share in the life that God promises. When told the reassuring news that it is precisely as he himself had said, that it was by *doing* God's will that people found life, the lawyer questioned the *interpretation* of that will: all right, he understands that in order to live he needs to love God with all the gifts God gives him, and his neighbour as himself; but 'who is my neighbour?' It's the same if we were to quibble about the other parts of the law: 'what does it mean to love myself', or 'how can I love God?'

At the heart of the story of the Good Samaritan stands the word 'doing'. 'What must I *do* to inherit eternal life?', the lawyer asked Jesus (Lk 10:25). And Jesus asks him about whether he has done what we were encouraged to do in the previous chapter: 'Have you read the Scriptures?', he asks, 'what do you read there?' The lawyer had faithfully studied the Scriptures, and explained them: 'You shall love the Lord your God with all your heart, and with all your soul, and with all your strength, and with all your mind; and your neighbour as yourself' (Lk 10:27). And Jesus assures the lawyer that it is this doing of God's will – loving God with all one's capacity and loving one's neighbour as oneself –

that shapes life in God's presence here and life forever in God's presence hereafter. 'You have given the right answer; do this, and you will live', Jesus assures his questioner (Lk 10:28).

The lawyer may have hoped for a simple formula to help him navigate his faith life. But Jesus reminded him that in order to live forever with him, which is what eternal life is, he needed to do more than formulaic following of God's commandments. In his case, the lawyer was told to let go of self-righteousness: the trait of self-justification of why the invitation to follow Jesus may be too complex, too ambiguous, too hard. In wishing to justify himself, he told Jesus that he loved God and neighbour as himself, but he didn't know who his neighbour was. Now Jesus tells him unambiguously that our neighbours are not restricted to one group of people, but that our neighbours may well be so radically different from us that (as in the case of the Samaritan) they hold different beliefs, they may not even believe in God at all.

We don't know how the lawyer responded. Where, in the last chapter, a rich young ruler walked away from Jesus grieving, this time Jesus walked away from the self-justifying lawyer. God's call means *doing* God's will, the story tells us, and questions separate us from God: even passively, as in this story of the lawyer from whom the Gospel story simply moves on.

Reflection: 'Do this and you will live'

'I can only learn what obedience is by obeying, not by asking questions.' (*Discipleship*, p. 76)

In reflecting on the Good Samaritan, Bonhoeffer refuses to allow us time to ask if someone is 'qualified' to be our neighbour. Everyone is our neighbour, or rather it is our job to act towards everyone as a neighbour.

In April 1933, only three months after the *Machtergreifung* (seizure of power), the Nazis incorporated the so-called 'Aryan Paragraph' in their *Law for the Restoration of the Professional*

Civil Service. The new law ruled that only Aryan people, that is people without Jewish parents or grandparents, could work in institutions administered by the German public service. By the end of April 1933, this law had been applied to universities and the German Protestant and Catholic Churches. In order to be no longer regarded as Jews, my own grandfather and great-uncle were baptised nine months after the laws were promulgated. At the time of their reception into the Lutheran Church they were in their mid-twenties. Their sudden conversion was of no avail: as people of Jewish descent they were still among those excluded from accessing tertiary education or holding public office under the 'Aryan Paragraph'.

The same held true for many German Protestant clergy of Jewish descent. As the Nazi 'Aryan Paragraph' was enforced among the German Church, the opponents of state sponsored racism, like Dietrich Bonhoeffer and Martin Niemöller, began to formalise their opposition to the Nazi German Christians. Bonhoeffer had been exposed to issues of racial persecution and social justice during his pre-ordination year at Union Theological Seminary in New York, which had consolidated his already strong pro-Jewish stance. At a synod in the Berlin suburb of Barmen in 1934, they established the Confessing Church. It was at least partly because Christians with Jewish parents or grandparents had been barred from university theological faculties that the Confessing Church began setting up underground seminaries in private estates, such as at Finkenwalde.

In his *Discipleship*, Bonhoeffer uses the story of the Good Samaritan to illustrate the point that it was wrong for the law to rule that certain people were not part of their community. Jews in Nazi Germany, like Samaritans in ancient Israel-Palestine, were legally excluded from the wider community. In the story of the Good Samaritan, Jesus makes clear that there are no outsiders among our neighbours: all people, regardless of their race or faith practise, must be included. And yet, we are all too often like the lawyer in this passage and want to quibble.

Dietrich Bonhoeffer suggests that it is not the principle of discipleship itself that is hard, but the motivation to do the actions of discipleship. In this chapter, we will be reflecting on the three possible responses people may make when God calls them into discipleship. We will examine what Bonhoeffer means by inadequate obedience and inadequate faith, and look at Bonhoeffer's charge to would-be disciples that following Jesus means taking up the cross.

The first response to Jesus' call is the right one, we reflected in the previous chapter when we looked at the stories of the calling of Levi and Peter and Andrew, James and John. The call is made and we obey and follow. Jesus came and called, the five left everything immediately to follow and share in that call. They made their immediate active response: they got up, left and at once followed Jesus.

The second response to God's call highlights what Bonhoeffer calls 'inadequate obedience'. It is shown well in the story of the rich young ruler we also looked at in the previous chapter. When invited by Christ to follow, he found it too hard to let go of his possessions and went away grieving the missed opportunity (Lk 18:18-23). The call is made, and we want to obey and follow, but the demands the 'doing part' of the call makes on us are too hard.

The third response to God's call is what Bonhoeffer calls 'inadequate faith'. It is the response shown in the story of the Good Samaritan. There are choices to be made, and those choices are active: are about acting in faith, are about doing God's will. The call is made, the doing part—'love God, love your neighbour as yourself'—is reinforced, and yet the lawyer sees an ambiguity in the command. He questions, 'who then is my neighbour' and, unable to accept the command, is left behind by Jesus. That is one of the slyest forms of disobedience to God's call, Bonhoeffer explains:

> What then happens is that people get so stubborn in their disobedience ... that they claim they can no longer discern

between what is good and what is God's command. They claim it is ambiguous and permits various interpretations.

The lawyer professes that he seeks to be obedient, but feels that God will not tell him how he can be so. Rather than seeking God, the lawyer is in fact running away from God. In many other places, people ask honest questions of Jesus, and he is generous in giving them answers, so we can see that this is not an honest question, but a question searching for a loophole.

Bonhoeffer reflects on the lawyer's questions: 'the question "What should I do?" is the first betrayal. The answer is: "Do the commandment that you know. You should not *ask*, you should *act*". The question "Who is my neighbour?" is the final question of despair or hubris, in which disobedience justifies itself. The answer is "You yourself are the neighbour. Go and be obedient in acts of love".'

In this way, Bonhoeffer believes, the lawyer is brought to judgment. He is called back from the question of salvation in general and instead confronted with the concept of simple obedience. Bonhoeffer asks: 'Why does he act as if he did not already know the answer to his question?' In acting this way, the lawyer is accusing God of withholding important information, according to Bonhoeffer, when all the information is already there but the lawyer is resisting acting on it.

Bonhoeffer here reinforces his understanding that the call to discipleship may only be answered by faithful obedience by doing the works of faith: 'I can recognise truth only by obeying.' The 'tempting scribe is shoved back to the commandment', returning to the law demands he acts according to the law. Responding to the call to follow Jesus, then, simply means doing what Jesus calls us to do. Responding to Jesus' call means following Jesus' commandments. And those commandments are given to us as an opportunity to do in practical terms what Jesus models. When we do the actions of faith, when we obey Jesus' call, we shift from the abstract beliefs of the lawyer – who professed that he had followed all of God's commandments throughout his life, who clearly knew what was required of him but failed to act on that knowledge – to the *practical* faith Jesus invites us to share through what we do.

Our doing the works of faith may lead us into places of danger and hardship. Some of us may be given the grace of martyrdom, as Bonhoeffer did himself. Many more of us will be given the grace of sharing in bearing the burden that is Christ's and ours, share in carrying the burdens of the sin and suffering of the world in which we live. And in this grace of suffering and death lies our life. 'Those who lose their lives in discipleship, in bearing the cross', Bonhoeffer told the trainee pastors of the Confessing Church, 'will find life again in following in the community of the cross with Christ.'

Why do we bear the burdens of others? Because Christ bore our own burdens, and now invites us to bear the load of others for his sake. Why do we lose ourselves in the shared carrying of the cross? Because Christ lost himself so that we might be saved. The call to discipleship is a call to carry the burdens of others, is a call to let go of our own self-interest, our self-justification, in order to share the burdens of our world. As Bonhoeffer says, 'the world's suffering needs a bearer', not an individual but the whole Church together.

We are called to be each other's neighbours, to bind each other's wounds, to take care of each other. This is also how we help others in the world who are suffering. It should be impossible to tell who is our fellow Christian and who is not, they are all our neighbours and they are all cared for by us.

Questions: Following Christ's Call

When we follow Christ's call as disciples, faith becomes a quality, an action; a vocation that we take on ourselves and actively live out. Faith becomes a practise and discipline of actions that gives shape to our faith. God gifts us this practise of the 'doing aspects' of our faith.

1. In 'Prayer in a Time of Hardship', Bonhoeffer sees himself as the man on the side of the road, for 'great misery has overcome me', and asks God to take care of him. How would his experience have been changed if more people were Good Samaritans?

2. In the Bible reading, the lawyer is keen to make sure that not everyone counts as his neighbour. Jesus' response suggests that our neighbour is the one who does us mercy, rather than the person who lives near us, shares our religion, our nationality or our culture. What would you, or your community, do differently if we saw 'neighbours' in this light?

3. Bonhoeffer says, 'Do the commandment that you know.' Which commandment is the one you already know, but keep asking about, rather than acting on?

4. How are you thinking about responding to what Jesus asks you to do? Listen to how other people in the group responded to God's call in their lives: What did they find costly and how did being with other believers or feeling close to God help them through those hard times?

5. The law is about loving God and loving your neighbour as yourself. What does it feel like to be loved? Think about what it would feel like to love yourself as you love God, and then show it to yourself. How can you share that love with others in concrete acts of goodness and mercy?

Prayer 'Help me to love you with all my heart'

Father in heaven,
help me to love you with all my heart:
let me serve you with all my strength,
and long for you with all my soul.

Help me to recognise your Son in those around me:
let me be a neighbour to those who need me,
and love myself and others as you love me.

Help me shoulder the cross that you have in store for me,
knowing that I carry it
alongside you and my neighbours. Amen.

Notes on: Following Christ's call

Image Attribution: Auszug aus dem Haftbuch des Zellengefängnis
Lehrter Straße, das am 23. April 1945 geschlossen wurde. Ausgestellt
in der Gedenkstätte Deutscher Widerstand. Public Domain.

Prayer in a time of hardship: 'Gebet in besonderer Not', Bonhoeffer,
Widerstand und Ergebung, p. 208.

I can only learn what obedience is by obeying: Bonhoeffer, *Discipleship*,
p. 75.

Inadequate obedience: Bonhoeffer, *Discipleship*, p. 78.

Inadequate faith: *Discipleship*, p. 78.

**What then happens is that people get so stubborn in their
disobedience:** *Discipleship*, p. 68.

The question 'What should I do?' is the first betrayal: *Discipleship*, p.
76.

Is already caught and brought to judgement: *Discipleship*, p. 76.

If the questioner is standing directly before God: *Discipleship*, p. 70.

I can recognise truth only by obeying: *Discipleship*, p. 76.

Those who lose their lives in discipleship, in bearing the cross:
Discipleship, p. 89

Christians become bearers of sin and guilt for other people: *Discipleship*, p. 88

The church community itself knows now that the world's suffering seeks a bearer: *Discipleship*, p. 90.

When Jesus commands: *Discipleship*, p. 78.

Prayer in a time of hardship: 'Gebet in besonderer Not', Bonhoeffer, *Widerstand und Ergebung*, p. 208.

Do the commandment that you know: *Discipleship*, p. 76.

Chapter 3: Costly Grace

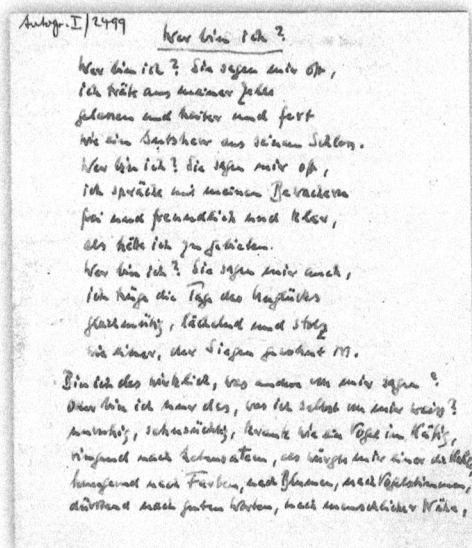

Handwritten letter from Bonhoeffer to Eberhard Bethge with text of 'Wer bin ich?' ('Who am I?'), July 1944. Photograph: Staatsbibliothek zu Berlin, Germany.

'Who am I?' (July 1944)

Who am I? They often say to me,
I step out of my cell
serene and cheerful and steadfast,
like a lord stepping out of his palace.
Who am I? They often say to me,
I speak with my guards
freely and friendly and clear,
As if I commanded them.
Who am I? They also say to me,
I bear the bad days
serenely, smiling and proud,
like someone used to victories.
Am I truly like what other people say about me?
or am I only what I know about myself?
Anxious, longing, sick, like a bird in a cage,
fighting for breath, as if someone were choking me.
Hungry for colour, for flowers, for birdsong,
thirsty for good words, for human closeness,
shaking with anger over the arbitrary
tyrannies and pettiest offences,
worried by the waiting for big things,
powerless and fearful about friends endlessly far away,
tired and empty of prayers, of thoughts, of creativity,
faint and prepared to take all my farewells.
Who am I? This or that?
Am I today this, then, and tomorrow something else?
Am I both at the same time? In front of people a hypocrite
and in front of myself a contemptible, whiny weakling?
Or, in the same way, which is still in me, the beaten army
that in disorder gives way in front of the
victory that has already been won?
Who am I? These solitary questions mock me.
As well: who I am, You know me, Yours am I, O God!

Bonhoeffer Reading:
'Our struggle today is for costly grace'

Cheap grace is the mortal enemy of our church. Our struggle today is for costly grace. Cheap grace means grace as bargain-basement goods, cut-rate forgiveness, cut-rate comfort, cut-rate sacrament; grace as the church's inexhaustible pantry, from which it is doled out by careless hands without hesitation or limit. It is grace without a price, without costs. It is said that the essence of grace is that the bill for it is paid in advance for all time. Everything can be had for free, courtesy of that paid bill. The price paid is infinitely great and, therefore, the possibilities of taking advantage of and wasting grace are also infinitely great. What would grace be, if it were not cheap grace?

Discipleship, p. 43

Further reading: read Chapter 1 of Bonhoeffer's *Discipleship*, pp. 46-76.

Bible Reading: 'The Lost Sheep and the Lost Coin'

[1]Now all the tax collectors and sinners were coming near to listen to Jesus. [2] And the Pharisees and the scribes were grumbling and saying, 'This fellow welcomes sinners and eats with them.' [3] So he told them this parable: [4] 'Which one of you, having a hundred sheep and losing one of them, does not leave the ninety-nine in the wilderness and go after the one that is lost until he finds it? [5] When he has found it, he lays it on his shoulders and rejoices. [6] And when he comes home, he calls together his friends and neighbours, saying to them, "Rejoice with me, for I have found my sheep that was lost." [7] Just so, I tell you, there will be more joy in heaven over one sinner who repents than over ninety-nine righteous persons who need no repentance. [8] Or what woman having ten silver coins, if she loses one of them, does not light a lamp, sweep the house, and search carefully until she finds it? [9] When she has found it, she calls together her friends and neighbours, saying, "Rejoice with me, for I have found the coin

that I had lost." [10] Just so, I tell you, there is joy in the presence of the angels of God over one sinner who repents.'

Luke 15:1-10

The Bible Reading in Context

The parables of the lost sheep and the lost coin are about searching for lost souls, caring more for the lost item than the many items that are safe. If God's grace is abundant, limitless, surely one coin or sheep would not matter? But the 'sinner who repents' is the person who hears Jesus' call and immediately rises up and follows him. And the rejoicing in heaven and the angels in the presence of God is for the 'one sinner.' This is costly grace, grace that God (as shepherd or woman) must work hard for, where every single sinner, sheep or coin is counted and valued. If limitless grace is careless and wasteful, these parables show us what God thinks grace is worth.

The two brief parables we consider in this chapter are about what it means to be found by Christ. The stories of a shepherd leaving behind a flock of ninety-nine sheep to search out one lost sheep, and that of a householder woman turning her home upside down in search of a single coin, are stories that teach us about the extravagant nature of Christ's love, and the assiduity of Christ in searching out the lost. They show us that God loves in ways that are more generous, more risk taking and more sacrificial than our own: the shepherd leaving behind ninety-nine sheep to look after themselves is not the most risk mitigating way of setting out to rescue a lost member of the flock.

They also show us how tireless Christ is in his seeking for those who are lost: raking through the dust and debris of our spiritual homes in the same way in which the householder woman cleaned out every nook and cranny of her own. Bringing light into all the dark spaces of our existence so that we may be found even in the murkiest shadows.

I wonder whether we wish to be found in this way, whether

we wish for our lives to be turned upside down by Christ? I wonder what it might feel like to be part of the ninety-nine sheep who are left behind, in order for the shepherd to go out and search for the one sheep that is lost? What it is like to have been found, raked over, and then be left to get on with the business of discipleship with the rest of the flock while Christ searches out others? I suspect there would be a sense of loss when the attention of the good shepherd shifted on other lost ones, and we were left to get on ourselves.

Our reading tells us that Christ is extravagantly generous in searching out those who need finding, and that Christian living is holding in balance, both the sense of rejoicing over a sheep found, and the sense of loss as the shepherd sets out to search for, call and bring in other lost sheep. The shepherd's abundant generosity and joy, and the flock's sense of loss, is costly grace.

Costly grace is the grace we receive when we let our lives be transformed by the encounter with the living God who came to look for us, leaving behind the ninety-nine others. Costly grace is the grace by which we are caught up in the broom of the living God, who sweeps away the darkness and mess of our sin and instead offers us order and life. 'It is the call of Jesus Christ, which causes a disciple to leave his nets and follow him.'

Reflection: 'I have found what I lost'

'Which one of you, having a hundred sheep and losing one of them, does not leave the ninety-nine in the wilderness and go after the one that is lost until he finds it?' (*Lk* 15:4)

The abundant, extravagant love of God comes at a price. Consequently, we should expect that our own loving, our own following too, will have a cost, a price. Christians call the life-giving love of God 'grace'. A love that overflows so that all may share in love. A love that is made visible in the life of Jesus Christ, who freely shared it with the self-righteous and the rich as much as with beggars and sinners. A love that was raised up on the cross, when Jesus gave his life freely, so that all may share in grace, may experience God's love. A love that is given for all, a love that is available through all ages and there for you and me today. That love comes at a price, the Scriptures tell us, and is radically different from human love.

At the heart of Dietrich Bonhoeffer's writings on Christian discipleship, composed for the students of his underground seminary of the German Confessing Church, stands a reflection on the cost of grace. 'What cost does grace have?', Bonhoeffer asks. And conversely, 'What does it mean to cheapen grace?' There is a clear line in Bonhoeffer's thinking between extending Christ's invitation to come and follow him to all people, and telling all people that they are all right in what they believe. The two, for Bonhoeffer, are utterly incompatible: we pour away Christ's love when we confirm others in their unbelief. Because belief is costly, following Christ comes with a price. In his lectures Bonhoeffer asked:

> Is the price we are paying today with collapse of the organised churches anything else but an inevitable consequence of grace acquired too cheaply? We gave away preaching and sacraments cheaply, performed baptisms and confirmations; we absolved an entire people, unquestioned and unconditionally; out of human love we handed over what was holy to the scornful and unbelievers.

Even in Bonhoeffer's time, many churches were finding they were losing members and becoming less relevant to their communities. Unlike the extremely successful African-American Abyssinian Baptist Church that Bonhoeffer attended in New York, the church in Germany was being replaced by political parties as the guide to life, family and society. The reason why the church is in decline, Bonhoeffer argued 80 years ago, was because 'we poured out rivers of grace without end, but the call to follow Christ rigorously was seldom heard.' There is, then, a difference between a positive inclination towards faith in general and the specific call to follow Christ. The former, Bonhoeffer argues, would still suit the people we considered in our previous chapters. Neither the rich young ruler nor the lawyer who asked Jesus about his neighbour were opposed to faith as a *principle*. Indeed, both of them professed that they lived by the precepts of faith. But neither of them were able to let go of the *one more* thing that was needed in order truly to follow Jesus; the things that preoccupied them even more than living by the precepts of faith, like wealth or the need to be right and righteous. The way of the lawyer and the rich young ruler, who seek to follow without giving up what holds them tied to the ways of the world, Bonhoeffer would argue, is the way of cheap grace.

'Cheap grace means justification of the sin and not the sinner', Bonhoeffer explains. It is true that grace is given freely, and accomplishes all in our life of faith. But this should not be an excuse for those who have been caught up in the life of grace to remain inactive, or worse still, reject the necessary change that comes with Christian living. If we do so, Bonhoeffer is convinced, the world remains in the grip of evil and people in sin.

'Cheap grace is grace without discipleship, grace without the cross, grace without the living, incarnate Jesus Christ', Bonhoeffer concludes. Cheap grace would allow the lawyer and the rich young man to live their established lives, even though they turn their back on the one who calls them to come and follow him. Cheap grace would forgive and forget self-righteousness rather than divine righteousness, temporal living rather than eternal life. The young man retains his riches, wipes away his tears of frustration of not being able to follow and nevertheless carries on living. He has received his reward. The lawyer remains self-justified and has received his reward. Neither of them change, they do not pay the price of costly grace. Bonhoeffer says it would be cheap grace to give them grace anyway.

What then is the cost of grace? What is grace worth? Jesus'

parables of the lost sheep and the lost coin, which we consider in this chapter, offer us two perspectives on the extravagant cost of God's love.

Luke tells two stories of loss and finding, of giving time and care, of diligence and risk taking, of leaving behind all in order to become a disciple. Both are little vignettes, opening a window into the heart of God. Both are introduced by a possibility of choice for the hearer: 'which of you, having a hundred sheep and losing one of them, does not leave the ninety-nine in the wilderness and go after the one that is lost' (Lk 15:4). Which of you does not react in this extravagant way, Jesus asks? This is not a rhetorical question expecting the answer, 'everyone will, of course', because clearly not everyone will act in this way. Leaving behind ninety-nine sheep in the wilderness, where they are likely to come under attack from all the kinds of dangers that are to be found there, is not a logical way to go out and mount a rescue operation. Most shepherds would cut their losses, Jesus implies, and leave the one sheep behind for the sake of the welfare of the whole flock. Indeed, the Pharisees are sensible community leaders who chose to lose the one lost sheep in order to maintain the integrity of the flock (Lk 15:2). This will be precisely their argument to justify asking for Jesus' crucifixion, 'it is better for you to have one man die for the people than to have the whole nation destroyed' (Jn 11:50). There is no costly risk-taking among them, and there is also no rejoicing. Just as in the stories of the rich young ruler and the lawyer, Jesus gives them a choice. 'Which of you would not react in this way?', he asks, expecting them to say, 'we wouldn't, actually.'

Yet the extravagant love of God is such, Jesus tells us, that he would leave behind *all* his sheep in order to search out the one. And then, having searched and left the flock to its own devices, find the lost animal, place it on his shoulders and give a great feast for his friends. 'There will be more joy in heaven over one sinner who repents', Jesus tells his hearers, 'than over ninety-nine righteous persons who', like the Pharisees who listen to the story, 'need no repentance' (Lk 15:7). The righteous may share in the rejoicing that others are brought to righteousness. But the righteous may not rejoice in their own righteousness. God's love calls us to leave the flock behind, and search diligently for that which was lost. And to share with joy with all in the conversion of the lost by feasting together. The Pharisees' grumbling, 'this fellow welcomes sinners and eats with them' (Lk 15:2), stands in stark contrast to the shepherd's joyful invitation, 'Rejoice with me, for I have found my sheep that was lost' (Lk 15:6).

Jesus continues to press home his point that God's love is costly. He asks his hearers which of them would not be like the woman, who 'having ten silver coins, if she loses one of them, does not light a lamp, sweep the house and search carefully until she finds it?' (Lk 15:8). Again, Jesus does not expect the answer: 'all of us.' Few people, in fact, is the answer to his question. The woman goes to incredible efforts to find the one coin: turning the house upside down, bringing light into the dark corners, sweeping it out – all to find what has been lost. Likewise, Jesus turned the house of Israel upside down, bringing light to the darkness of sin, sweeping away self-righteousness, for example in the Cleansing of the Temple (Lk 19:45-46). Not many are like that woman, certainly not those whose interest lies in preserving the status quo. If you don't want your life, your home, turned upside down by a busybody householder who forensically searches through everything, shines light into our darkness, then following Jesus may not be for you, Bonhoeffer suggests. Jesus brings light and order to the house, that is true. But that light and order comes at the cost of breaking all the habits that prefer darkness and mess. The coin is found, the house swept clean where people allow Jesus into their homes and lives and, in the same way, 'there is joy in the presence of the angels over one sinner who repents' (Lk 15:9).

We know that God counts the value of coins differently

from humans. When Jesus observed people bringing gifts to the Temple treasury, he pointed out a widow who gives two copper coins. Compared to the rich people, who gave much larger amounts, it is she who 'has put in more than all of them; for all of them have contributed out of their abundance, but she out of her poverty has put in all she had to live on' (Lk 21:2-4). A God who counts value not by size or number but by total commitment might well go after one sheep, one coin, one soul.

Remember our first reflection in which Levi gave a banquet for Jesus and invited all his colleagues along? Then Jesus had explained to the grumbling Pharisees, 'I have come not to call the righteous, but sinners to repentance' (Lk 5:32). Jesus' call then had been successful: those who found themselves on the margins of faith, who did not try and quench their thirst from the rivers of cheap grace, came and were transformed by Jesus' call to believe and follow. They now drank deeply from the waters of new birth. However, the Pharisees held tight to their lives lived by their narrow precepts, and resented the One who called sinners to repentance with such extravagance.

This is costly grace. It costs us our habits, our comfort, our all, Bonhoeffer explains (quoting Mt 13:45-46, and Mt 5:29): 'costly grace is the hidden treasure in the field for the sake of which people go and sell with joy everything they have. It is the costly pearl for whose price the merchant sells all that he has; it is Christ's sovereignty, for the sake of which you tear out an eye if it causes you to stumble'.

Why is it costly? Because it costs God much to show such extravagant love to those who are lost – think of the shepherd leaving behind his flock. Because it costs the lost their previous lives – think of the tax collector leaving behind his livelihood, the fishermen their nets, business, even their family and employees. It also costs the community of those who already follow Jesus, when they are no longer the priority of a shepherd more interested in, perhaps more needed by, a lost soul.

Bonhoeffer concludes his observation of the cost of being found: 'It is costly, because it calls us to discipleship; it is grace because it calls us to follow Jesus Christ. It is costly because it costs people their lives; it is grace because it makes them live. Above all, grace is costly, because it was costly to God, because it costs God the life of God's Son.'

This extravagant love is offered to us freely by the God who lets go of all in order to call us, find us and bring us home if only we let ourselves be found by him, and follow faithfully where he leads.

The call to discipleship is first of all a call to self-denial. We are to put ourselves second and Jesus first in order to follow. Now the disciples are told that in order to follow Jesus, they like him will need to face rejection and embrace suffering; even death. Not just once, but daily. Jesus tells them: 'If any want to become my followers, let them deny themselves and take up their cross daily and follow me' (Lk 9:23). Discipleship means denying ourselves daily, taking up our cross daily, and following. When we follow, we are not left to our own devices. Even though each response is an individual response to follow, when we do become disciples of Jesus, we join a community of believers. We join a community of others who do what we do: listen out for Jesus' call to us, doing what he asks us to do, letting go of those things in which we need to deny ourselves. We share with others in shouldering the cross.

Questions: Costly Grace

Grace may be given freely, Bonhoeffer argued, but it comes at a price: it costs us our settled lives, and it costs God, the giver of all life, the life of his Son Jesus Christ.

1. In his poem 'Who am I?', Bonhoeffer is like the woman with the lost coin, shining a light into his dark places, including reflecting on some things are also strengths and gifts, like his charm and graciousness. Which of your strengths are like the light that casts a shadow?

2. Bonhoeffer was a pacifist who believed that lying, war, murder and killing were absolutely wrong and against God's laws, but also that it was absolutely the right thing to do to become a double agent and to conspire to assassinate Hitler. What do you think it cost him to give up his principles for what he believed to be the greater good?

3. These parables are about the lost soul, but many people are already part of God's community. What does it feel like to be a part of the ninety-nine sheep in the wilderness as the shepherd sets out to seek the lost? Does the grumbling of the Pharisees strike a chord in you, standing at the fringes of God's banquet looking in on the sinners and tax collectors and thinking, 'this fellow welcomes them and eats with them'? Or do you bear one another's burdens? How does your community celebrate someone accepting God's grace in their life?

4. Bonhoeffer reflects that grace-lived discipleship 'is costly because it costs people their lives.' For Bonhoeffer and hundreds of his first readers, that was literally true. What do you think of a discipleship that could cost so much?

5. God's love is also entirely free. Do we personally, or in our community, require people to strive to deserve grace, when grace comes freely? Do you exert 'strength, effort and discipline which is unnecessary, even dangerous, since everything is already prepared and fulfilled by grace'?

Prayer 'Brought home at a cost'

I am yours, O Lord,
A sheep searched for in your care,
Found and brought home to your fold.
I am yours, O Lord,

A sinner swept clean by your grace,
Redeemed and bought at the price of your life.
I am yours, O Lord,

A disciple called by your Word,
Set free to rejoice in doing your will.

Let me be yours, O Lord,
When you leave me behind
and set out to search for my neighbour.

Let me be yours, O Lord,
When you return again with joy
and heaven echoes your delight at finding us.

Let me be yours, O Lord,
When you come at the end of all time,
to bring in your judgement of mercy and grace.

Amen.

Notes on: Costly Grace

Image Attribution: Dietrich Bonhoeffer, Staatsbibliothek zu Berlin, Autograf I/2499. Scan from Facsimile. Public Domain.

Who am I: 'Wer bin ich?', Bonhoeffer, *Widerstand und Ergebung*, p. 513-14.

It is the call of Jesus Christ: *Discipleship*, p. 44.

Is the price we are paying today with the collapse of organised churches: Bonhoeffer, *Discipleship*, p. 53.

We poured out rivers of grace without end: *Discipleship*, p. 53.

Cheap grace means justification of sin and not the sinner: *Discipleship*, p. 42.

Because grace does everything: *Discipleship*, p. 42.

Cheap grace is grace without discipleship: *Discipleship*, p. 42.

Costly grace is the hidden treasure: *Discipleship*, p. 44.

It is costly, because it calls to discipleship: *Discipleship*, p. 44.

It is costly because it costs people their lives: *Discipleship*, p. 44.

Strength, effort and discipline which is unnecessary: *Discipleship*, p. 54.

Who am I: 'Wer bin ich?', Bonhoeffer, *Widerstand und Ergebung*, p. 513-14.

It is costly because it costs people their lives: *Discipleship*, p. 44.

Strength, effort and discipline which is unnecessary: *Discipleship*, p. 54.

Chapter 4: Christ's Call and the Cross

Destruction in a Berlin Street from aerial bombing.
Photograph: Sergeant A Wilkes, No 5 British Army
Film and Photographic Unit, 1945.

Christians and Heathens (July 1944)

The people go to God in their distress,
Pleading for help, begging for happiness and bread,
For salvation from sickness, trespasses and death.
Everyone does this, everyone, Christians and Heathens.
The people go to God in their distress,
Find him poor, vilified, without shelter or bread
See him devoured by sin, frailty and death,
Christians stand with God in his suffering.
God goes to all people in their distress,
Satisfies body and soul with his bread.
For Christians and Heathens, he dies the death on a cross
And forgives both.

Bonhoeffer Reading: 'The cross is suffering with Christ'

The cross is neither misfortune nor harsh fate. Instead, it is that suffering which comes from our allegiance to Jesus Christ alone. The cross is not random suffering, but necessary suffering. The cross is not suffering that stems from natural existence; it is suffering that comes from being Christian. The essence of the cross is not suffering alone; it is suffering and being rejected. Strictly speaking, it is being rejected for the sake of Jesus Christ, not for the sake of any other attitude or confession. A Christianity that no longer took discipleship seriously remade the Gospel into only the solace of cheap grace. Moreover, it drew no line between natural and Christian existence. Such a Christianity had to understand the cross as one's daily misfortune, as the predicament and anxiety of our natural life. Here it has been forgotten that the cross always also means being rejected, that the cross includes the shame of suffering. Being shunned, despised, and deserted by people, as in the psalmist's unending lament, is an essential feature of the suffering of the cross, which cannot be comprehended by a Christianity that is unable to differentiate between a citizen's ordinary existence and Christian existence.

The cross is suffering with Christ. Indeed, it is Christ-suffering.

Discipleship, p. 86

Further reading: read Chapter 4 of Bonhoeffer's *Discipleship*, pp. 84-91.

Bible Reading: 'Peter's Confession'

[18] Once when Jesus was praying alone, with only the disciples near him, he asked them, 'Who do the crowds say that I am?' [19] They answered, 'John the Baptist; but others, Elijah; and still others, that one of the ancient prophets has arisen.' [20] He said to them, 'But who do you say that I am?' Peter answered, 'The Messiah of God.' [21] He sternly ordered and commanded them not to tell anyone, [22] saying, 'The Son of Man must undergo great suffering, and be rejected by the elders, chief priests, and scribes, and be killed, and on the third day be raised.' [23] Then he said to them all, 'If any want to become my followers, let them deny themselves and take up their cross daily and follow me. [24] For those who want to save their life will lose it, and those who lose their life for my sake will save it. [25] What does it profit them if they gain the whole world, but lose or forfeit themselves? [26] Those who are ashamed of me and of my words, of them the Son of Man will be ashamed when he comes in his glory and the glory of the Father and of the holy angels.'

Luke 9:18-26

The Bible Reading in Context

Our Scripture reading takes us to a pivotal moment in the relationship between Jesus and his disciples. They knew Jesus to be a powerful preacher and healer. They had seen him feed thousands of people with a few loaves and fishes. They had witnessed him still a storm and bring to life a dead young man. Now Peter realises that he is more than a mighty prophet who has arisen. Jesus is greater than Elijah or John the Baptist. He is 'the Messiah of God', Peter confesses (Lk 9:20). God's own anointed One. The One who would bring in God's rule. God's promised Saviour, who would set things right: bringing in justice, restoring faith, calling people to turn again to the Lord their God.

Jesus disabuses Peter and the eleven of any ideas that his kingship would be anything other than the rule of suffering. He explains to them that God's Messiah ('the Son of Man' foretold in the prophet Daniel) 'must undergo great suffering and be rejected by the elders, chief priests and scribes and be killed, and on the third day be raised' (Lk 9:22). The Son of Man would indeed eventually be seated at the right hand of glory, as prophesied by Daniel (Dan 7:13-14). But first he would embrace rejection, suffering and death. And his disciples would be called to do the same.

At the same time, Jesus gives his followers the promise of good things beyond the value of a 'good life' in this world. By following Jesus, taking up their cross even unto death, the disciples are saved from a worse fate: they will not 'lose or forfeit themselves' and they will not be 'ashamed' in the glorious second coming. Everyone will one day die, it doesn't matter if you take up your cross or not. But not all will be treated with honour by the Son of Man when he comes in glory.

Reflection: 'Take up your Cross and Follow me'

'The cross is not random suffering, but necessary suffering.' (*Discipleship*, p. 86).

Following Jesus means rejection and suffering. It means shouldering daily the cross that Christ himself bears, Jesus tells his disciples. In return for this act of bearing the cross, the disciples are promised a community of others and community with Christ who both share in the bearing of it. Where we shoulder the cross, we deny our own self-interests and instead join a community of cross-bearers. We share with Jesus and all other disciples in bearing the cross that he himself bore. It is in this shared bearing that we are enabled to undertake the daily task of denial of self in order to follow Christ.

Dietrich Bonhoeffer makes a sharp distinction between suffering and rejection. Only one of the two carries shame. In his *Discipleship*, Bonhoeffer writes: 'Jesus Christ has to suffer and be rejected.' We can glory in suffering, receive sympathy and compassion for embracing suffering and hardship. But we will never be admired for being rejected or turned away. Rejection goes well beyond suffering, takes away any admiration, any sympathy, Bonhoeffer knows: 'Rejection removed all dignity and honour from his suffering. It had to be dishonourable suffering.'

It is the removal of honour that Jesus invites his followers to enter into. Taking up our cross daily means to face suffering and rejection, and so to share in our own lives something of the crucifixion of Christ. Bonhoeffer explains: 'Just as Christ is only Christ as one who suffers and is rejected, so a disciple is a disciple only in suffering and being rejected, thereby participating in crucifixion.' By following Jesus, we assent daily to sharing with him rejection and suffering. We conform daily to the new commandment of love shown forth supremely on the cross.

Bonhoeffer told the students of his underground seminary in Finkenwalde that following Jesus is a pledge of allegiance to suffering and rejection. We are given a new commandment, that of radical inclusive love, when we follow Christ. This law of love and compassion will set disciples at odds with the world. Bonhoeffer's students at Finkenwalde were well aware of the very practical implications of their decision to break with the Nazi Reich Church and enter into active opposition: 'Discipleship as allegiance to the person of Jesus Christ places the follower under the law of Christ', Bonhoeffer told them, and pointed to the end point of their journeys of discipleship: 'that is it places the follower under the cross.'

Even the first to hear Jesus' call, those fishermen who heard Jesus' personal invitation to come and follow him, found this scandalous. In Matthew's Gospel we read how Peter, upon hearing Jesus tell them that he is to be rejected, is to suffer and to die, rebukes him. 'God forbid it, Lord', Peter tells, 'this must never happen to you' (Mt 16:22). Peter here voices what we all might feel. It is scandalous, offensive that Christ should be rejected, should be dishonoured, should be murdered.

Dietrich Bonhoeffer explains that, from the beginning of the church's story, right there from the moment in which Jesus proclaimed Peter the rock on which he would build his church, it has been difficult to accept that suffering and rejection, self-denial and death to self are an integral part of our faith. 'The fact that it is Peter, the rock of the church, who makes himself guilty doing this just after he has confessed Jesus to be the Christ and has been commissioned by Christ, shows that from its very beginning the church has taken offense at the suffering Christ', Bonhoeffer writes.

But following Christ places us, his followers, into the same position. We may be dishonoured, rejected, even face death for following the rejected Messiah. Bonhoeffer understands that Peter's offense is only partly about being offended for Jesus' sake. He is also offended because he does not want to be rejected, dishonoured or murdered. As Bonhoeffer writes, 'Peter's objection is his aversion to submit himself to suffering.' While this may seem an understandable feeling, Bonhoeffer is uncompromising. We cannot try to avoid suffering because 'that is a way for Satan to enter the church.'

For Bonhoeffer, the temptation to avoid rejection is a fundamental problem which was clearly mirrored in the theology of glory of the Nazi Reich Church. A church that is tempted by glory and comfort is not a church that shares and embraces the suffering of its Lord: 'It does not want that kind of Lord, and as Christ's church it does not want to be forced to accept the law of suffering from its Lord.' This temptation is a temptation to evil. For Bonhoeffer, the leaders of the Reich Church's glorification of Hitler, their glorification of the Aryan race and their avoidance of suffering were what directly caused the violence and exclusions against their political opponents, people of other races, and Confessing Church pastors. It is not only that avoiding suffering made the church complicit in the state violence of the government it supported. In attempting to avoid suffering or defeat, the Reich Church directly participated in that violence. When the Gestapo closed down Finkenwalde, it was on the advice of the Reich Church authorities.

Bonhoeffer had himself faced the temptation to avoid suffering. He could have stayed in the USA in 1939 but returned to Germany. He had many other opportunities to escape later, when he was travelling internationally as a double agent it would have been easy to disappear to safety. Instead, Bonhoeffer decided, and continued to decide, to take up his cross and accept the suffering that was in front of him.

And yet, for Bonhoeffer, 'suffering' does not mean unremitting torment, and accepting that suffering may come does not mean seeking out acts of self-martyrdom or ascetic exercises. Instead it means freedom from the fear of suffering. If we are not afraid of suffering, of losing our possessions, of looking foolish—then we cannot be imprisoned in those things. What then are we called to do as people who want to answer Jesus' call to discipleship? We hear and respond to Christ's call by listening to his Word and discerning his will for us. We allow ourselves to be searched out and found by him. And now we are called to allow ourselves to be set free from our own selves in order to follow wholeheartedly. Bonhoeffer put it this way: 'Therefore, once again, before the law of discipleship is proclaimed, even the disciples must accept being set free.'

The freedom from yourself does not mean replacing yourself with a void. It means replacing yourself with *knowing Christ*. In German, Bonhoeffer uses the verb *kennen* here. German has two verbs for 'to know': *wissen*, which is closer to 'knowing about', the kind of knowing that comes from learning about something;

and *kennen*, the kind of knowledge that comes from personal relationship and experience. We do not *know about* Jesus, we truly know him in relationship. 'Self-denial means knowing only Christ, no longer knowing oneself.' Taking this step means changing your perception, your view, what you see in the world. Self-denial 'means no longer seeing oneself, only him who is going ahead.'

For Peter, being ashamed of Jesus turned out to be more painful than accepting that he would 'forfeit' himself. The Gospel stories tell us that the experience of what it means to deny self was a hard lesson for Peter. He was the first who confessed Jesus to be the Messiah. Yet as Jesus was being sentenced to death in the courtyard of Pilate's palace he also denied Christ three times. Bonhoeffer tells us: 'Just as in denying Christ Peter said, "I do not know the man", those who follow Christ must say that to themselves.' Christians are called to deny themselves and lose themselves for Christ's sake: it was when Peter became willing to lose his life for Jesus' sake that he found salvation and forgiveness.

After Jesus' resurrection, Peter affirmed his discipleship three times, John tells us in the final chapter of his Gospel (Jn 21:15-19). By the lake of Galilee, three times Peter affirmed his desire to follow in the same sacrificial way that Christ modelled. Three times he declared that his love for Christ was greater than anything else. Sitting next to the greatest haul of fish he had ever caught, Peter confessed that his love for Jesus was greater than his successful fishing business. In turn, Jesus charged him to 'feed my lambs' (Jn 21:15). Peter next affirmed that his love was greater than the love for his own needs and, in turn, Jesus commanded him to become the kind of shepherd who ceaselessly searches out the lost. Finally, Peter affirmed that his love was even greater than the love for his own life. In turn, Jesus charged Peter to nurture Christ's flock until death and prophesied that he would die in his service.

Peter's later affirmations are more hard-won than his

confession of Jesus as Messiah in this week's reading. Jesus knows what is coming, and warns his listeners: 'If any want to become my followers, let them deny themselves and take up their cross daily and follow me. For those who want to save their life will lose it, and those who lose their life for my sake will save it. What does it profit them if they gain the whole world, but lose or forfeit themselves? Those who are ashamed of me and of my words, of them the Son of Man will be ashamed when he comes in his glory and the glory of the Father and of the holy angels' (Lk 9:23-26).

This denial of self through the daily letting go of those things that deter us from following Christ can be painful. But Bonhoeffer tells us we will also be given immense strength: 'If Jesus had not been so gracious in preparing us for this word, then we could not bear it. But in this way he has made us capable of hearing this hard word as grace.'

The Melbourne-based New Testament theologian Brendan Byrne puts this well: denial of self means the daily decision to face the 'loss of the "life" created by the self's own superficial desires in order to gain the life that fulfils the self's deepest longings—to love and be loved, to give and receive a communion of love—both human and divine.'

The decision to follow Jesus is one that is made daily, the Gospel tells us. Even if we have already made the fundamental commitment to enter into discipleship ourselves, we daily need to recommit to and reorient ourselves towards Christ and his cross. This is what Byrne calls 'spirituality for the long haul.' It requires us to take the cross that is already there for us and bear it, and to do so every day. Bonhoeffer reminds us that that it is our own cross to bear, which will be just right for us. 'But so that no one presumes to seek out some cross, or arbitrarily search for some suffering, Jesus says, they each have their own cross ready, assigned by God, and ready to fit.'

No-one may judge how much someone else can or should

suffer. 'Everyone gets a different amount' of suffering, so that our cross is one we can carry. For each one of us, our suffering is given according to who we are, Bonhoeffer believes. In a moment of prescience of his own death seven years later, that caused me to shiver when I read it, he said: 'God honours some with great suffering and grants them the grace of martyrdom, while others are not tempted beyond their strength.' Together we suffer in community, in it together, Bonhoeffer continues, because 'in each case, it is the one cross.'

Questions: Christ's Call and the Cross

Bonhoeffer encouraged us to take up our cross and follow Christ's call in obedient faith:

> A Christian becomes a burden-bearer. ... As Christ bears our burdens, so we are to bear them. When we have really forgotten ourselves completely, when we really no longer know ourselves, only then are we ready to take up the cross for his sake. When we know only him, then we also no longer know the pain of our own cross.'

1. In his poem 'Christians and Heathens', Bonhoeffer reminds us that when we go to God with petitions for 'happiness and bread', we ask it of a God on a cross 'poor, vilified, without shelter or bread', and yet, that God gives us his Son and the bread of heaven. What does it feel like to be forgiven for wanting salvation from death?

2. In the story of the confession of Peter, Jesus says, 'Those who want to save their life will lose it, and those who lose their life for my sake will save it' (Lk 9:24). What would you do differently if you, or your community, were not afraid for your life?

3. At the time of writing his *Discipleship*, Bonhoeffer was a pacifist and committed to non-violence. He was strongly opposed to deaths in war, by violence, forcible euthanasia, execution, or genocide. Later, he came to believe that the assassination of Hitler was necessary, but only to avoid further deaths. What does it mean to hold life valuable, but yet believe it might be something to give up?

4. What is the cross-shaped burden in your own life, or your community's life, that you need to shoulder at this time? What may it be that you need to face – being rejected or dismissed for by others – in order to be true to the call of Christ?

5. Bonhoeffer says the suffering of the cross is 'not random suffering'. Do we sometimes mistake 'random suffering' which happens to everyone for the 'necessary suffering' of the cross? How can we tell the difference?

Prayer 'Scandalous Salvation'

You were made an outsider for me, Lord,
were rejected, mocked and spat upon,
so that I might learn patient endurance.

You carried the cross for me, Lord,
were tortured, and killed lifted on high,
so that I might learn to bear burdens.

You are a stumbling block for me, Lord,
were placed on my way, straight in my path,
so that each time I fail, I fall on you.

Amen.

Notes on: Christ's Call and the Cross

Image Attribution: No. 5 Army Film & Photographic Unit, Wilkes A. (Sergeant). Creative Commons.

Christians and Heathens: 'Christen und Heiden', Bonhoeffer, *Widerstand und Ergebung*, p. 515.

Jesus Christ has to suffer and be rejected: Bonhoeffer, *Discipleship*, p. 84.

Rejection removed all dignity and honour: *Discipleship*, p. 85.

Just as Christ is only Christ as one who suffers: *Discipleship*, p. 85.

Discipleship as allegiance to the person of Jesus Christ: *Discipleship*, p. 85.

The fact is that it is Peter: *Discipleship*, p. 85.

Peter's objection is his aversion to submit himself to suffering: *Discipleship*, p. 88.

That is a way for Satan to enter the church: *Discipleship*, p. 88.

Therefore, once again: *Discipleship*, p. 86.

Self-denial means knowing only Christ, no longer knowing oneself: *Discipleship*, p. 86.

Means no longer seeing oneself, only him who is going ahead: *Discipleship*, p. 86.

Just as in denying Christ: *Discipleship*, p. 86.

If Jesus had not been so gracious in preparing us for this word: *Discipleship*, p. 86.

Loss of the 'life' created by the self's superficial desires: Brendan Byrne, *The Hospitality of God: A Reading of Luke's Gospel*, Liturgical Press, Collegeville, 2015, p. 88.

Spirituality for the long haul: Byrne, *The Hospitality of God*, p. 88.

But so that no one presumes to seek out some cross: *Discipleship*, p. 87.

Everyone gets a different amount: *Discipleship*, p. 87.

God honours some with great suffering: *Discipleship*, p. 87.

A Christian becomes a burden-bearer: *Discipleship*, p. 86.

Poor, vilified, without shelter or bread: *Widerstand und Ergebung*, p. 515.

Chapter 5: Becoming Followers

Picture of Flossenbürg concentration camp, Bavaria, where Bonhoeffer was imprisoned and executed. Photograph: US Army 99th Infantry Division April 1945

Evening Prayer (November 1943)

Lord my God,
I thank you for bringing this day to its end.
I thank you for letting body and soul come to rest.
Your hand was over me, and sheltered and preserved me.
Forgive all my little faith and all the wrongs of this day
and help me to gladly forgive them
who have done wrong to me.
Let me sleep in peace under your cloak
and guard me from the temptations of darkness.
I commend to you all who are mine
I commend to you this house,
I commend to you my body and soul.
God, your holy name be praised,
Amen.

Bonhoeffer Reading: 'Discipleship and the Individual'

Jesus' call to discipleship makes the disciple into a single individual. Whether disciples want to or not, they have to make a decision; each has to decide alone. It is not their own choice to desire to be single individuals. Instead, Christ makes everyone he calls into an individual. Each is called alone. Each must follow alone. Out of fear of such aloneness, a human being seeks safety in the people and things around them. Individuals suddenly discover all their responsibilities and cling to them. Under their cover, they want to make their decision, but they do not want to stand up alone in front of Jesus, to have to decide with only Jesus in view. But at that moment neither father nor mother, neither spouse nor child, neither nation nor history cover a person being called. Christ intends to make the human being lonely. As individuals they should see nothing except him who called them.

Discipleship, p. 92

Further reading: read Chapter 5 of Bonhoeffer's *Discipleship*, pp. 92-99.

Bible Reading: 'Give up all your possessions'

[25]Now large crowds were travelling with Jesus; and he turned and said to them, [26] 'Whoever comes to me and does not hate father and mother, wife and children, brothers and sisters, yes, and even life itself, cannot be my disciple. [27] Whoever does not carry the cross and follow me cannot be my disciple. [28] For which of you, intending to build a tower, does not first sit down and estimate the cost, to see whether he has enough to complete it? [29] Otherwise, when he has laid a foundation and is not able to finish, all who see it will begin to ridicule him, [30] saying, "This fellow began to build and was not able to finish". [31] Or what king, going out to wage war against another king, will not sit down first and consider whether he is able with ten thousand to oppose the one who comes against him with twenty thousand? [32] If he cannot, then, while the other is still far away, he sends a delegation and asks for the terms of peace. [33] So therefore, none of you can become my disciple if you do not give up all your possessions.'

Luke 14:25-33

The Bible Reading in Context

In previous chapters, we saw how those who chose to follow Jesus followed knowing full well that Christ called them not to a life of holy introspection, but a life of active doing in his name. Very early on in their journeys with Jesus, they were told that the end-point of both his journey and theirs would be a place of rejection and suffering. That, in following, they would face death. We reflected that this suffering would not be the honourable suffering that attracts the praise or pity of the world, but a suffering that was dishonourable, even disreputable. For when Jesus calls women and men, he calls them to suffer rejection with him.

The first experience of suffering for those who are called, is the cutting of their accustomed ties, we learnt in our reflections.

Peter, Andrew, James and John, the first to follow Christ's call, left behind their livelihood, property and families. In the same way, we need to be ready to cut off ties or, as Bonhoeffer calls it, to burn bridges. 'The first Christ-suffering that everyone experiences is the call which summons us away from our attachments to this world', Bonhoeffer tells us. That severance of relationships and letting go of habits, the hating of anything and anyone who is not Christ, is in itself a form of dying. 'It is the death of the old self in the encounter with Jesus Christ', Bonhoeffer knows: 'Those who enter into discipleship enter into Jesus' death. They turn their living into dying; such has been the case from the very beginning.'

In the parable of the Great Banquet (Lk 14:15-23), which immediately precedes our reading, Jesus had taught large crowds about God's extravagant love and generous hospitality. God's kingdom was like a large feast, where there was not only abundant food but place aplenty at the table. There was in fact so much room, that God had to send out for more people to fill any empty seats: 'Go out to the roads and country lanes and compel them to come in, so that my house will be full', Jesus tells in the parable of the Great Banquet (Lk 14:23). God is generous, and God's kingdom is a place of incredible hospitality.

All people are invited, Jesus had just explained in his parable. But each person needs to accept the invitation to celebrate with God. And each one of us does so by herself or himself. The invitation is a matter between the individual and God. It cuts right across any other ties we already have. 'Whoever comes to me and does not hate father and mother, wife and children and even life itself, cannot be my disciple', Jesus tells the large crowds that were attracted by his teaching (Lk 14:26).

Jesus then proceeds to tell the people that following him has a cost. He counsels them that they should consider carefully whether following is for them before they make their commitment. In two short parables, he speaks about the cost of discipleship in terms of an ambitious building project and a planned conquest. In both cases, Jesus tells his listeners, people first evaluate their resources before setting out to build, or to wage a war. Successful builders of a tower first estimate the cost and then set out to build. In this way, they fulfil their ambition and, at the end, receive praise and not derision, Jesus tells: 'If you lay the foundation and are not able to finish it, everyone who sees it will ridicule you, saying, "This fellow began to build and wasn't able to finish"' (Lk 14:30).

Discipleship is a life-long commitment, Jesus is saying here. Before we commit, we too should consider whether we are able to embark on the costly journey of daily carrying the cross and following Jesus. In Bonhoeffer's case, he was choosing to set out to wage a war and build an edifice he knew he was likely to lose in this world. But he knew the greater battle had already been won by Christ, and that he would only be on the winning side if he made peace with carrying his cross.

We all respond individually, but we all follow together. That, we think, may be a help in unlocking Jesus' rather uncompromising charge to aspiring disciples to 'hate father and mother, wife and children, brothers and sisters, yes—and even life itself' which we will consider in more detail in this chapter (Lk 14:26).

Reflection: 'Do not love your world'

Individuals suddenly discover all their responsibilities and cling to them.' (*Discipleship*, p. 92)

In order to follow Jesus, we need to put Jesus before anything or anyone else. The Son of God comes first, and then those he entrusts us to care for, and to care for us. There is a place for family relationships in God's kingdom. But Christ is the head of the family and comes first. Dietrich Bonhoeffer explains that when we recognise Christ as the Son of God, the mediator, we have to loosen our ties with the world that surrounds us. This does not mean that the relationships we are called to no longer matter. They do. But they are mediated by Christ.

When answering the call of Christ, we do so alone, not as part of a family, or as part of a partnership. Each of us need to take the decision to discipleship as individuals. Bonhoeffer explains: 'Jesus' call to discipleship makes the disciple into a single individual. Whether disciples want to or not, they have to make a decision; each has to decide alone.' This is why St Paul exhorts us to pray for our partners (1 Cor 7:12-16), so that they, too, may be enabled to make the decision we each are called to make. 'Each is called alone. Each must follow alone.'

When we respond to Christ's invitation, we are to consider carefully whether the call to discipleship is for us. In each of the stories of call and response we consider in this book, we see how Christ leaves room for a genuine decision. Individuals are each given the opportunity to reject the invitation, are given space for the realisation that following Jesus is not for them. That is a fair response to Jesus' call: not all will follow. But all are called. If having their lives turned upside down by Jesus, if having their ties of relationships and occupation disrupted by Jesus is not for them, people need not follow. But those who do accept Jesus' call, need to put Jesus above all.

Bonhoeffer explains: 'Jesus' call itself already breaks the ties with the naturally given surroundings in which a person lives … Christ has untied the person's immediate concern with the world and bound the person immediately to himself.' We rightly ask ourselves why we need to be alone in order to focus on Christ? Bonhoeffer responds: 'Christ intends to make the human being lonely. As individuals they should see nothing except him who called them.' It is when we are aware of that aloneness that we realise the closest relationship we can have is with God. As Bonhoeffer wrote in his 'Morning Prayer' (which we considered in Chapter 1), 'I am lonely, but you do not leave me.' It is impossible for a human being to avoid ever being left by another. In human relationships, we constantly move away and return, until we move away from this life through death. But God is able to be with us always.

However, this does not mean that we should never work to be in relationship with other humans; simply that we should do so through Christ. If Christ truly is to be the mediator between God and humankind, the mediator of the new covenant of love, then Christ needs to mediate all relationships. Bonhoeffer told the students at Finkenwalde Seminary that this is precisely the point of the Incarnation, the point of God becoming human in Christ Jesus: 'In becoming human, Jesus put himself between me and the given circumstances of the world.' In fact, 'he is in the middle' between Bonhoeffer and the rest of the world. When Christ calls, he cuts all ties. 'All bridges had to be burned', Bonhoeffer expressed it in his reflection on the call of Levi. And that exclusivity of calling – when Christ calls, we either love him and follow or reject him and stay behind – leads to the stark language of 'hating' the world around us, 'even life itself' (Lk 14:26). If life with Christ is our goal, then life is not worth living if we are apart from Christ. Only with Christ is life worth living, and family ties worth sustaining, our Gospel reading tells us. Because the moment I commit to following Christ, he stands between me and everything else.

Dietrich Bonhoeffer put it this way:

> Jesus wants to be the mediator; everything should happen only through him. He stands not only between me and God. He also stands between me and the world, between me and other persons, but also between person and person, and between person and reality.

For the followers of Christ, Christ is the mediator through whom we regard everything else in life. If we follow him, then we love him. And in the same binary pattern that underlies so much of Jesus' teaching, when we love one thing, we cannot also love another thing.

'Whoever comes to me, and does not hate father and mother, wife and children, brothers and sisters, yes, and even life itself, cannot be my disciple' (Lk 14:26). Followers love the one who calls them. When we become followers, we love Jesus first and hate all relationships that are not mediated by Christ. If anyone or any ideology prevents us from standing as individuals before Christ, responding individually to his call, then we need to make a decision to turn towards, or away from, Christ. If we truly turn to Christ, then we need to shun those who claim to be alternative mediators. And that is what 'hating' the world means.

You see, Jesus does not tell his disciples that they cannot love their families through him. In fact, when the apostle Peter ask him precisely this question, Jesus responds that those who love him first will reap a harvest of love, will actually gain family ties. Peter said, 'Look, we have left our homes and followed you.' Jesus responded, 'Truly I tell you, there is no one who has left house or wife or brothers or parents or children, for the sake of the kingdom of God, who will not get back very much more in this age, and in the age to come eternal life' (Lk 18:29-30).

For Levi, the rich young ruler, the lawyer and the fisherman— their profession or wealth or identity stood between them and following Jesus, they could not keep both. In the parables we considered in the previous chapters, the shepherd and the woman ignore everything else to search for the lost soul, and find the thing that is worth rejoicing over.

In stories in the Acts of the Apostles, following Jesus and having him at the centre is shown to be possible for families, married couples, communities and workplaces who value each other and their labour through Jesus, through their discipleship.

The idea that the followers of Jesus may relate to the world apart from their discipleship is alien to Bonhoeffer. 'Immediacy is a delusion', he tells us.

The most loving sensitivity, the most thoughtful psychology, the most natural openness do not really reach the other person—there are no psychic immediacies. Christ stands between them. The way to one's neighbour leads only through Christ.

How can we relate to each other through Christ? Just as Christ intercedes for us, so our concern for one another, our love for one another, is best expressed through intercession, Bonhoeffer tells us: 'That is why intercession is the most promising way to another person. And common prayer in Christ's name is the most genuine community.'

When Christ mediates all our relationships, our vertical relationship with God and our horizontal relationships with those we care for and those we entrusted to our careful concern, then we are united with God and one another through Christ. We may each have to respond alone to Christ's call. But once we have responded, we are expected to become a community in our shared love for Christ mediated by Christ's love.

Bonhoeffer puts it this way: although each one of us needs to respond as an individual to follow Christ's call, 'they find themselves again in a visible community which replaces a hundredfold what was lost. A hundredfold? Yes, the promise for those who follow Christ is that they will become members of the community of the cross; they will be people of the mediator, people under the cross.'

Knowing the endpoint of our following sets into perspective the demands made of us. We will only ever be able to sustain the journey to the cross when Christ stands between us and suffering and rejection. We will only ever be able to shoulder the cross when we love Christ, and walk in his strength. And we will only ever receive his strength through the mediated community of faith of the members of his own body.

This also means that when we live in community, we always need to be thinking how we can be Christ to other people. Helping them carry their burdens, just as they help us carry ours. This means giving one another peace, rest, joy, healing and security, the very things that Bonhoeffer asks for in his intercessions.

When Bonhoeffer lived in community at Finkenwalde, he led the ordinands in intellectual debates, prayer and silent meditation; but also in sing-a-longs, walks in the woods, holidays and meals together. Bonhoeffer was known for his sense of humour, his approachable manner and his authenticity. In prison, he was known for his charm, his calmness, his graciousness. These are also things that we should give one another, mediated through Christ's love, care and companionship with us.

Those who follow will receive infinitely more than that which they leave behind, Jesus answers the disciples who ask themselves whether their sacrifice has been of value. But of far greater value is the sacrifice of the one who loved us first and called us. Bonhoeffer quotes John 3:16 to make his point: "God so loved the world that he gave his only Son, so that everyone who believes in him may not perish but have eternal life."

Questions: Becoming Followers

Bonhoeffer tells us that Jesus seeks to be our mediator and that everything should happen only through him. He reminds us that Jesus stands between each individual and God, between each individual and other persons, and between person and reality.

1. In his 'Evening Prayer', Bonhoeffer writes: 'I commend to you all who are mine, / I commend to you this house, / I commend to you my body and soul.' How might you use prayer to help Jesus to be the mediator of love between you and your family, surroundings, mind and physical being?
2. The Bible reading recommends we count the full potential cost of discipleship before setting out. How would you count what it costs to be a disciple? How does that accounting impact your planning for your journey with Christ?
3. Has the call of Christ led you to new relationships and

friendships, new communities? How does Jesus mediate between you and old relationships, friendships and communities?

4. What would it be like to love and be loved only through Christ? What actions would you take if you did not have to strive for love? What actions would you take if you were challenged to act through Jesus' love for others?

5. What would it mean if the people and things around you were reasons to respond to Jesus' call, and not reasons why it was too hard to follow him?

Prayer 'Mediated by your love'

Father, set your Son Jesus Christ between me and my loved ones:
that I may see them as he sees them,
and love them with his love.

Set your Son Jesus Christ between me and my community:
that I may pray for them as he prays for them,
and care for it with his care.

Set your Son Jesus Christ between me and my world:
that I may serve it as he serves it,
and forgive as he forgives.

Set your Son Jesus Christ between me and my judgement,
that I may shoulder my cross as he shouldered his,
and be freed from death by his death. Amen.

Notes on: Becoming Followers

Image Attribution: US Army 99th Infantry Division April 1945. Public Domain..

Evening Prayer: 'Abendgebet', Bonhoeffer, *Widerstand und Ergebung*, p. 207.

Jesus' call to discipleship: Bonhoeffer, *Discipleship*, p. 92.

The first Christ-suffering that everyone experiences is the call: *Discipleship*, p. 87.

It is the death of the old self in the encounter with Jesus Christ: *Discipleship*, p. 87.

Those who enter into discipleship enter into Jesus' death: *Discipleship*, p. 87.

Individuals suddenly discover all their responsibilities and cling to them: *Discipleship*, p. 92.

Jesus' call to discipleship makes the disciple into a single individual: *Discipleship*, p. 92.

Each is called alone. Each must follow alone: *Discipleship*, p. 92.

Jesus' call itself already breaks the ties: *Discipleship*, p. 93.

Christ intends to make the human being lonely: *Discipleship*, p. 92.

I am lonely, but you do not leave me: Bonhoeffer, *Widerstand und Ergebung*, p. 204-205.

In becoming human, Jesus put himself between me: *Discipleship*, p. 93.

He is in the middle: *Discipleship*, p. 93.

All bridges had to be burned: *Discipleship*, p. 58.

Jesus wants to be the mediator: *Discipleship*, p. 94.

Christ the mediator stands between son and father: *Discipleship*, p. 95.

Immediacy is a delusion: *Discipleship*, p. 96.

That is why intercession is the most promising way: *Discipleship*, p. 96.

They find themselves again in a visible community: *Discipleship*, p. 99.

I commend to you all who are mine: *Widerstand und Ergebung*, p. 207.

Chapter 6: Being Christ's Body

Handwritten letter from Bonhoeffer to Maria von Wedemeyer with text of 'Von guten Mächten' ('By good forces'), 19 December 1944. Photograph: Houghton Library, Harvard University, USA.

By good forces loyally and silently surrounded
(December 1944)

By good forces loyally and silently surrounded,
Miraculously shielded and consoled:
So I will live these days with you
And go with you all into a new year.

Yet the old year will still torment our hearts,
Yet the evil days will still weigh heavy on us.
Oh Lord, give us untroubled souls,
The salvation that you have won for us.
And you extend to us the heavy chalice, the bitterness,
The suffering, filled right up to the brim—
So we take it from you, with thanksgiving, without trembling,
From your good and beloved hand.

…

Let the candles flame warm and bright,
That you have brought into our darkness.
When it is possible, lead us together again!
We know it, your light shines in the night.

…

By good forces miraculously made secure,
Confidently awaiting what is to come.
God is with us in the evening and the morning
With complete assurance for every new day.

Bonhoeffer Reading:
'Anyone who fears God is no longer afraid of people'

Human beings should not be feared. They cannot do much to the disciples of Jesus. Their power stops with the disciples' physical death. The disciples are to overcome fear of death with fear of God. Disciples are in danger, not from human judgment, but from God's judgment, not from the decay of their bodies, but from the eternal decay of their bodies and souls. Anyone who is still afraid of people is not afraid of God. Anyone who fears God is no longer afraid of people. Daily reminders of this statement are valuable for preachers of the Gospel. The power which is given to people for a short time on this earth is not without God's knowledge and will. If we fall into human hands, if we suffer and die by human violence, we may be sure that everything comes from God. God, who lets no sparrow fall to the ground without the divine will and knowledge, will not permit anything to happen to God's own people except what is good and useful for them and their cause (Lk 12:6-7). We are in God's hands. Therefore, 'be not afraid!' Time is short. Eternity is long. It is the time of decision. Those who remain faithful to the word and the confession here will find that Jesus Christ will stand by them in the hour of judgment. He will know them and stand with them when the accuser demands they be judged. The whole world will be witnesses when Jesus names our name before his heavenly Father.

Discipleship, p. 196-197

Further reading: read Chapter 7 of Bonhoeffer's *Discipleship*, pp. 183-198.

Bible Reading: 'Jesus' entry into Jerusalem'

[28] Jesus went on ahead, going up to Jerusalem. [29] When he had come near Bethphage and Bethany, at the place called the Mount of Olives, he sent two of the disciples, [30] saying, 'Go into the village ahead of you, and as you enter it you will find tied there a colt that has never been ridden. Untie it and bring it here. [31] If anyone asks you, "Why are you untying it?" just say this, "The Lord needs it."' [32] So those who were sent departed and found it as he had told them. [33] As they were untying the colt, its owners asked them, 'Why are you untying the colt?' [34] They said, 'The Lord needs it.' [35] Then they brought it to Jesus; and after throwing their cloaks on the colt, they set Jesus on it. [36] As he rode along, people kept spreading their cloaks on the road. [37] As he was now

approaching the path down from the Mount of Olives, the whole multitude of the disciples began to praise God joyfully with a loud voice for all the deeds of power that they had seen, [38] saying, 'Blessed is the king who comes in the name of the Lord! Peace in heaven, and glory in the highest heaven!' [39] Some of the Pharisees in the crowd said to him, 'Teacher, order your disciples to stop.' [40] He answered, 'I tell you, if these were silent, the stones would shout out.'

Luke 19:28-40

The Bible Reading in Context

We are almost at the endpoint of our journey. Jesus is about to enter the Holy City Jerusalem, there to complete his ministry on earth. This Bible reading takes us another step closer on that journey of 'living dying'. It takes us to the approach to Jerusalem where Jesus will face yet the harshest rejection by the authorities, where he will face arrest, a short and slanderous trial, and a long and cruel death. Jesus commands his disciples to prepare for his entry to Jerusalem. They bring a colt, clothe it with their garments, and 'set Jesus on it' (Lk 19:35). As he is guided into the city, people spread their cloaks onto the dusty road to make a carpet of garments. And all his followers, all those whom he had called from their previous attachment to the world, hail him as their ruler.

Here was the Messiah, the One who 'comes in the name of the Lord' (Lk 19:38). Here was the One who by his acts of power gave glimpses in this life of the true nature of the life to come. Here was the One who would embrace rejection and suffering, and lay down his life so that all who hear his call would have life forever. The disciples become joyful witnesses of Christ's works and call. As Jesus enters the Holy City on a road covered with palm branches and garments, they publicly affirm their confession of Jesus as the Christ, the Promised One.

Their song of praise makes an important distinction: in

heaven Jesus will bring peace and glory, 'peace in heaven and glory in the highest heaven', they sing (Lk 19:38). Yet on earth he will bring division and a sword (Lk 12:51).

Bonhoeffer expressed it this way: 'Who can claim the people's love and sacrifice so exclusively, if not the enemy of humanity or the Saviour of humanity? Who will carry the sword into their homes, if not the devil or Christ, the Prince of Peace?'

For the community leaders who demand Jesus make his disciples stop their testimony, Jesus is the enemy endangering their fragile peace and the fragile protections they enjoy under the rule of an oppressive empire. The authorities demand that the disciples voices be silenced: 'Teacher, order your disciples to stop', some Pharisees said to Jesus (Lk 19:39). But just as the daily struggle with the world is an integral part of the daily pattern of faithful discipleship, so the very fabric of the city is a living testament to the rejection of those sent there to save it. 'I tell you', Jesus rebukes the Pharisees, 'if these were silent, the stones would shout out' (19:40). The stones of the city would testify to the call of Christ to turn from the ways of this world to the peace and glory, the freedom and sanctuary of heaven. To the first readers of the Gospel story, these stones are not any old rocks. The stones are the very material of the land and the city of Jerusalem which they believed to be especially loved by God.

At the decisive moment, as Jesus enters the city, the disciples' testimony is to the kingdom and the life that lasts forever. They witness about what it has been like to follow Christ, to contend daily with evil and suffering. They witness about what it has been like to see Christ bring justice and peace, healing and grace to those who sought him out.

Reflection: 'Blessed is the King'

'Time is short. Eternity is long.' (*Discipleship*, p. 197)

Dietrich Bonhoeffer told the students at his underground seminary in Finkenwalde in unambiguous terms that their own discipleship would mirror Christ's: 'Whenever Christ calls, his call leads us to death', he put it starkly. The cross which is the endpoint of the journey of the One who calls is also the endpoint of the journeys of all those who follow: 'The cross is not the terrible end of a happy, pious life', Bonhoeffer knows: 'instead it stands at the beginning of our community with Jesus Christ.' This is true for all followers, not only those who, like Bonhoeffer and his students, followed Christ in times of adversity. From the moment a person follows the call of Christ, they receive the cross: 'the cross is laid on each Christian.'

When we witness to Christ through our words and actions, we bring Christ to the world, carry an inestimable gift to others. Disciples are 'bearers of Christ's presence', Bonhoeffer tells: 'They bring the people the most valuable gift, Jesus Christ, and with him, God, the Father, and that means forgiveness, salvation, life, blessedness. That is the reward and the fruit of their work and their suffering.' We are called to be a blessing to others, because we have received the blessing of Christ. Bonhoeffer tells us that when we do what Christ calls us to do, we become Christ-bearers to others: 'Those who carry Jesus' word receive one last promise for their work. They have become Christ's co-workers and helpmates.'

As disciples of Jesus, then, we are entrusted with showing forth the precious gift of Christ's own presence to our world, and we show forth that presence through our actions. We witness to the One who carries our cross by carrying one another's burdens. By sharing in shouldering the injustices others face, as well as by advocating and fighting on their behalf. And this aspect of witnessing has implications not only for life within the community of faith, but also for life in the society in which we live, particularly if that society oppresses its members.

Commenting on Christian living under the repressive Nazi regime, Bonhoeffer told his students at Finkenwalde, 'Where the world despises other members of the Christian family, Christians will love and serve them. If the world does violence to them, Christians will help them and provide them relief.' Here Bonhoeffer says, 'the world.' In other places he says 'the state', the government. If the 'world' feels too big, our local government is tangible and knowable. In the last chapter we looked at how Christ mediates our relationships to families and other individuals. Here we consider how Christ mediates our relationship to our society and its systems.

Who is supported by our government? Who is given justice? Who is valued and given official positions? If there are people who are excluded, can we include them? If there are people who are silenced, can we give them space to speak and amplify their voices? If there are people who are not given sufficient support, can we give them more? In this way, we work regardless of the many people who have made faith irrelevant in modern society, and regardless of the many people, perhaps even a majority, who slumber when others suffer. This is what Bonhoeffer and his colleagues in the Confessing Church worked to do in the 1930s and 1940s.

As followers of Jesus Christ, then, we cannot remain hidden, and leave the witnessing about the One who called us to 'the stones [of Jerusalem that] would shout out' (Lk 19:40). Nor can we leave the witnessing to the costliness of Christian discipleship to the war memorials located in the concentration camps of Flossenbürg and Buchenwald. Nor to the names of non-Jewish 'Righteous among the Nations' inscribed at Yad Vashem, the World Holocaust Remembrance Centre in Jerusalem. It is true that all these places (and many more the world over) serve as silent witnesses to the personal sacrifice of those who followed in the footsteps of Christ. They testify to those who gave their lives in order to carry the inestimable gift of Christ's presence into the suffering of our world. These stones will continue to shout and witness when our own voices are silenced. But if we are serious about our Christian discipleship, then we also need to make our voices heard. We need to speak out with those whose voices are being silenced. And that means standing up to unjust structures and rulers, as well as serving and tending to those who have become victims of such structures.

When the Nazis took power in early 1933, Bonhoeffer expressed the church's obligation in this way:

> When the church witnesses that the state exercises too much or too little order and justice, it is placed in the position not only of having to bandage the wounds of the victims beneath the wheel, but to drive a spoke into the wheel itself.

Bonhoeffer's opposition to anti-Semitism was not only moral, but also practical and active. He elaborated how the church would need to resist injustice and oppression. 'First, questioning the state as to the legitimate state character of its actions, that is, making the state responsible for what it does.' Especially in situations where there are close links between faith communities and those in power, or institutional norms that prioritise one faith community, then that community has a responsibility to hold the government to account when it oppresses others.

Bonhoeffer continues: 'Second is service to the victims of the state's actions. The church has an unconditional obligation toward the victims of any societal order, even if they do not belong to the Christian community.' Bonhoeffer quotes Galatians 6:10: 'Let us work for the good of all.' We need to become Good Samaritans to those abandoned by the state or by community leaders. We are not called to ask if the victims qualify as our neighbour.

We have an equally great responsibility when the state or community leaders have actually caused the violence or damage.

Recent Royal Commissions in Australia meticulously detailed how those in power in the state and the church damaged and ignored children, Indigenous people, victims of sexual assault and domestic violence, those with mental illnesses and many others. Bonhoeffer is clear that the church, the followers of Jesus, have 'an unconditional obligation' to serve all such people: those whom Jesus called 'the least of these' (Mt 25:40) because they are treated as 'least' by society.

These are both ways in which the church, in its freedom, conducts itself in a free state. In times when the laws are changing, the church may under no circumstances neglect either of these duties. Yet Bonhoeffer goes even further, 'The third possibility is not just to bind up the wounds of the victims beneath the wheel but to seize the wheel itself.' As the war approached, and the attacks against Jews increased, Bonhoeffer realised the church and its leaders could not, or would not, take the necessary stand against the terrors of the Nazi state. Martin Niemöller was in a concentration camp. Karl Barth and Franz Hildebrandt were in exile. Many other pastors and lay leaders who might have taken their places were in similar situations. For Bonhoeffer, and his family, seizing the wheel of the state meant gathering evidence of Nazi crimes, working with enemies of the German state like the United Kingdom and the United States of America, and plotting to overthrow the government. While Bonhoeffer did not start his political journey planning to 'seize the wheel', he was prepared to do so if his discipleship made that necessary.

As Jesus enters Jerusalem on his way to die on the cross for his followers, the disciples bear witness through their song of praise of how inextricably linked the realm of faith is with the affairs of our world. Heaven and earth are linked, they sing in their hymn 'Blessed is the king who comes in the name of the Lord! Peace in heaven, and glory in the highest heaven!' (Lk 19:38). They see in front of their eyes, here on earth, a heavenly king entering a city that is both a real place and a symbol of an eternal city.

'Those who remain faithful to the word and the confession here will find that Jesus Christ will stand by them in the hour of judgement. He will know them and stand with them', Bonhoeffer encourages us on our own journeys of courageous following. In the same way that Jesus' disciples witness to his deeds of liberating power, so Jesus will witness to them in the time of their trial and suffering. This is what true discipleship means: to stand by Christ in his suffering. Stand together by the members of the body of Christ in their suffering. The people who have heard and responded to his call, who have taken on their share of the cross in suffering and self-denial. The people who have confessed Jesus in this world are those with whom Jesus will stand forever.

When we live as disciples in this world, Jesus will help us bear our burdens of faith-filled living and sacrificial action in this world. Bonhoeffer assures us that when we witness to Christ in this world, he will bear witness for us in the world to come: 'Those who have held onto Jesus in this life will find that Jesus will hold onto them in eternity.'

Questions: The decision

When the Nazis came to power early in 1933 Dietrich Bonhoeffer knew that the church's response would need to be one of active opposition, holding the regime accountable for their actions, proactively caring for the victims of oppression. Bonhoeffer knew then that greater sacrifices might be called for: 'When the church witnesses that the state exercises too much or too little order and justice, it is placed in the position not only of having to bandage the wounds of the victims beneath the wheel, but to drive a spoke into the wheel itself.'

1. The assurance and togetherness Bonhoeffer writes about in the poem 'By good forces' was entirely spiritual. Bonhoeffer knew he was unlikely to survive the war, and yet he takes 'the heavy chalice' from God, with 'the suffering, filled right

up to the brim', and drinks it 'with thanksgiving, without trembling.' How can we carry on a form of 'living dying' that includes joy and 'complete assurance for every new day'?

2. In the Bible reading, Jesus directs his followers to unruly actions, they borrow a donkey without permission, the crowd disrupts the peace, and Jesus defies the religious authorities. Yet in other places, Jesus says we should render unto the emperor what is the emperor's and obey seemingly unjust laws. How does Bonhoeffer help us to think through when it is right to obey the state and when to challenge it?

3. How can we avoid being silent about Jesus Christ? How does your study group or faith community help you gain the tools and confidence to enable you to witness to Jesus' transforming power in your life?

4. How do you translate your words of witness into action? How will you endeavour to overcome evil with good? Are there causes your faith makes you passionate about, and taking positive actions to support?

5. What are the darknesses , the injustices of our age, that your church needs to stand up against? How will you let your voice be heard in your advocacy, your protest, your intentional voting and campaigning? Bonhoeffer was part of a movement of resistance: whom can you join with to bring mercy and justice to the world?

Prayer 'Agents of Christ's love'

Lord Jesus Christ,
My Friend and Brother,
grant me the strength to follow you when you call,
and the confidence to share with others the salvation
you have won for us.

Lord Jesus Christ,
My Saviour and my Judge,
grant me the courage to speak out when voices are silenced,
and the resolve to act in your name when evil days
weigh heavy on us.

Lord Jesus Christ,
my God and my King,
grant me the grace to walk alongside you
through our world,
so that I might be an agent of your transforming love

Amen.

Notes on: Being Christ's Body

Image Attribution: Dietrich Bonhoeffer, Autograph des Gedichts 'Von guten Mächten' in seinem Brief an Maria von Wedemeyer aus dem Kellergefängnis de Reichssicherheitshauptamts in Berlin, Prinz-Albrecht-Straße, 19. December 1944. Public Domain.

By good forces loyally and silently surrounded: 'Von guten Mächten', Bonhoeffer, *Widerstand und Ergebung*, p. 607-608.

That is the work of Christ on earth: *Discipleship*, p. 197.

Time is short. Eternity is long: *Discipleship*, p. 197.

Whenever Christ calls, his call leads us to death: *Discipleship*, p. 87.

The cross is not the terrible end of a happy, pious life: *Discipleship*, p. 87.

The cross is laid on each Christian: *Discipleship*, p. 87.

Disciples are bearers of Christ's presence: *Discipleship*, p. 198.

They bring the people the most valuable gift: *Discipleship*, p. 198.

Those who carry Jesus' word receive one last promise for their work: *Discipleship*, p. 198.

Where the world despises: *Discipleship*, p. 236.

When the church witnesses that the state: Bonhoeffer, 'The Church and the Jewish Question', *Berlin 1932-33*, p. 365.

First, questioning the state: *Berlin 1932-33*, p. 365.

Second is service to the victims: *Berlin 1932-33*, p. 365.

Unconditional obligation: *Berlin 1932-33*, p. 365.

The third possibility is not just to bind up the wounds of the victims beneath the wheel: *Berlin 1932-33*, p. 365.

Seize the wheel: *Berlin 1932-33*, p. 365.

Those who remain faithful to the word: Bonhoeffer, *Discipleship*, p. 197.

Those who have held onto Jesus in this life: *Discipleship*, p. 197.

When the church witnesses that the state: Bonhoeffer, 'The Church and the Jewish Question', *Berlin 1932-33*, p. 365.

By good forces: 'Von guten Mächten', Bonhoeffer, *Widerstand und Ergebung*, p. 607-608.

Beyond the book: Authors' reflection

Martin Luther King, Oscar Romero and Dietrich Bonhoeffer, sculptures on the West Façade of Westminster Abbey, London UK. Photograph: Cristian Bortes.

Night-time voices (July 1944)

Stretched out on my pallet-bed,
I stare at the grey wall.
Outside, a summer morning—
That is no longer anything to do with me—
is progressing, rejoicing into the countryside.
Brother, after this long night,
Our day will break.
We hold our ground.

Authors' Reflection:

High on the south-west tower of St Paul's Cathedral Melbourne, facing over one of the busiest intersections of the city, is an orange and white banner that says 'Let's Fully Welcome Refugees.' We put up the seven-metre banner in August 2013, just before an election where both major political parties used harsh asylum seeker policies in seeking to win or retain power. Their slogan was 'Stop the Boats.' Together with the Brotherhood of St Laurence, the Cathedral recommended specific policies advocating for a more compassionate refugee policy. However, the purpose of the banner was to go beyond just raising target numbers or adjusting working rights. It was to say that refugees would not be fully welcome in our community until we accepted them with love, until they became our neighbours.

In the six years since we put up the banner, Australia's offshore detention centres have become more and more obviously concentration camps. Islamophobia and anti-immigration sentiment have become more mainstream, its representatives have been elected into parliament and are routinely being broadcast on television. Around the world, people are looking to the Second World War for inspiration, whether for harsh new policies against 'others' or for paths to resistance.

Around the world, we see German grandmothers regularly marching against neo-Nazis (Andreas' mother goes often in her home city of Munich). We see Jewish Americans standing outside border camps with signs reading 'Never again' (the motto is a cry to never allow another Holocaust) on the news. We see families in the United Kingdom opening their homes to refugees fleeing the conflicts in the Middle East; even the Archbishop of Canterbury has opened his London home, Lambeth Palace, to a Syrian refugee family.

Here in Melbourne, every year on Palm Sunday (and throughout the year, in response to the news), people gather to protest about Australia's response to refugees: Protestants, Catholics, Jews, lawyers, doctors, communists, trade unionists, children, families, individuals, communities and faith groups. St Paul's Cathedral is there every year, with clergy and congregation marching with palm branches, palm crosses, banners and signs as a sign that we cannot afford to leave the proclamation of Christ's radical love to the stones of Jerusalem.

At the same time, St Paul's Cathedral welcomes refugees. The Cathedral holds free English language classes followed by a fellowship meal, offered regardless of a refugee's religion, need or ability to pay. We welcome refugees who have come to faith after coming to Australia, who join our community through Bible study, baptism and confirmation. We also welcome refugees who have fled their homeland because of their Christian faith, who join the congregations and take on leadership positions. If we only welcome refugees when we can be their benefactors, that is not truly living in community with them. We also welcome refugees when they give us hospitality, when they lead us. We listen when they teach us.

We are not finished in this work of living together. We are also aware that there are many other causes that need equal attention: the work of reconciliation with Indigenous peoples and the work of repairing the damage done to the environment are two examples if a long list.

When Andreas gave the sermon series that led to the

reflections in this book, he had many people coming up to him afterwards to say how much Bonhoeffer inspired them. Many retired people reflected on how Bonhoeffer's witness had turned them towards lives of mercy, liberation and service. Many young people were just learning about Bonhoeffer for the first time, and were amazed by how relevant his story was to the challenges they saw in their world.

When Katherine gave the lecture that led to the biography and translations in this book, she really struggled to find the right way to end it. This is what she said then, and it probably stands as how we would like to end this book too:

And so we come to the end of our reflections on Bonhoeffer, on captivity and freedom.

On the one hand, we see that Bonhoeffer's captivity was literal. That the freedoms of speech, of religion, of association, of political views that we assume are fundamental human rights in a liberal democracy can come under threat and be taken away in a few short years.

We see how fragile our own political and religious freedoms are, when we look at how, even here in Australia, there is a harsher rule for Indigenous people under the 'Intervention' in the Northern Territory and another for Indigenous people living in the south; how there is a harsher rule for asylum seekers arriving by boat and another for asylum seekers arriving by plane. In such a situation, how secure are the rules we might take for granted?

Even in captivity people like Bonhoeffer and those in his circle refused to collaborate with their oppressors. That Bonhoeffer does not stop working for, or longing for, the double freedom that he believed would come. The freedom of Germans when the Nazis were removed from power, whether that was done from within by protest, conspiracies and coups; or from without by the Allied forces 'liberating' the country. And the other, greater, freedom of eternal life with God.

And both of these freedoms are not freedoms of ease and prosperity, of jobs and tax cuts; rather 'When Christ calls a man, he bids him come and die.'

As I came to end the talk, and as we come to end this book, we couldn't shake the sense that the *Letters and Papers from Prison* reminded us of something. Something about a man who seemed to have an uncanny stature, calmness and grace under incarceration, a book that was smuggled out of prison in electronic messages of philosophy, resistance and poetry... and coming to realise that we must listen to the martyrs and prophets in our midst, who speak to us from prison. The recently published memoir *No Friend But the Mountains* is written by the Iranian-Kurdish journalist, human rights activist, poet and film producer, Behrouz Boochani, who is still on Manus Island. His book reminds us that today we must fight for the freedom of those our country currently declares not quite whole persons, in order that we don't end up in history on the wrong side of it.

Notes on: Beyond the Book – Authors' reflection

Image Attribution: Cristian Bores. Creative Commons 2.0.

Stretched out on my pallet bed: 'Langgestreckt auf meiner Pritsche', from: 'Nächtliche Stimmen', Bonhoeffer, *Widerstand und Ergebung*, p. 516.

Never again: Talia Lavin, 'When Non-Jews Wield Anti-Semitism as Political Shield', GQ.com, 17 July 2019, https://www.gq.com/story/anti-semitism-political-shield.

When Christ calls a man, he bids him come and die: 'Whenever Christ calls, his call leads us to death', *Discipleship*, p. 87.

Recommended Further Reading

If you have been inspired by this book to find out more, here are some good places to start.

Books by Bonhoeffer:

Letters and Papers from Prison: Dietrich Bonhoeffer, edited by Eberhard Bethge, *Letters and Papers from Prison,* Schuster and Schuster, New York, 1992.

The Cost of Discipleship, Dietrich Bonhoeffer Works 4, edited in German by Martin Kuske and Ingrid Tödt, and edited in English by Geffrey D. Kelly and John D. Godsey, tr. by Barbara Green and Reinhard Kraus, Augsburg Fortress Press, Minneapolis, 2001.

Read more about Bonhoeffer:

The Cambridge Companion to Dietrich Bonhoeffer, ed. John W. de Gruchy, Cambridge University Press, Cambridge, 1999.

Dietrich Bonhoeffer: Called by God, Elizabeth Raum, Continuum, New York and London, 2002.

Elizabeth Sifton and Fritz Stern, *No Ordinary Men: Dietrich Bonhoeffer and Hans von Dohnányi – Resisters against Hitler in Church and State,* New York Review Books, New York, 2013.

Read more about Luke's Gospel

Brendan Byrne, *The Hospitality of God: A Reading of Luke's Gospel,* Liturgical Press, Collegeville, 2015.

About the translation

Bonhoeffer's German is delightfully clear, straightforward and modern. His craft is clear in the poems, prayers and hymns he writes. His close familiarity with liturgy and the Bible means that he occasionally uses a more archaic form, but one that would nevertheless be perfectly understandable and familiar to his audience. Where the poetry is straightforward in German, I have rendered it straightforwardly into English. Where it echoes the form of the Psalms or uses a word from the Lord's Prayer, for example translating 'Schuld', which can mean debts or sins, as 'trespasses.' Typically, I have used the same English word to translate the same German word ('wunderbar' is always 'miraculous') but not at the expense of straightforwardness and understanding.

Not every sentence in the poetry is completely crystal clear. Sometimes Bonhoeffer puts words together unexpectedly or in a way that might have two meanings—something that modern poetry is designed to be able to do. Where the poetry is unclear, or has potential multiple meanings, I have written it in English in a way that will probably mean the reader needs to stop and think for a moment about what is happening there.

In English, Bonhoeffer's literary cousins would be Ernest Hemingway or WH Auden; in German, poets like Berthold Brecht. I wanted the translation to have something of the same texture. Like Brecht, or Auden, Bonhoeffer's language often has a double meaning, clear to anyone who was listening. This is something that, Raum argues, Bonhoeffer had learned to do when preaching in Berlin in the 1930s, as speaking publicly against the Nazi regime was made illegal. Nonetheless, by keeping close to the Biblical texts, Bonhoeffer was able to make his points. In a similar way, when his whole family would meet to discuss their resistance, they developed a form of code in case they were overheard.

The same is true in his poems, which are never directly about wanting to be rescued by Allied forces, or hoping that the von Stauffenberg plot would be successful, but serve to reassure his readers that he was holding his ground against the interrogations, that he hoped for the right kind of ending.

For this reason, I have translated 'Von guten Mächten' differently from many other versions. *Letters and Papers from Prison* has, 'With every power of good to stay and guide me', and *Love Letters from Cell 92* choses to render to the poem 'By kindly, faithful, tranquil powers surrounded.' Hilmar H. Werner translates this line and the following: 'By loving forces silently surrounded/ I feel quite soothed, secure, and filled with grace.' However, I see the 'Mächten' as both the forces of God's love and the 'Allied Forces', only a few weeks away from liberating Germany from the east and the west. So the language in my translation is quite different: 'By good forces loyally and silently surrounded, / Miraculously shielded and consoled.'

Bonhoeffer's poems are sometimes in free verse, sometimes in strict hymn rhyme and metre, sometimes a mixture of both. I have chosen not to try to reproduce the rhythm or rhyme of the originals, as I suspect the readers of this book are more interested in what Bonhoeffer meant—theologically, politically, personally. On the whole, though, I have tried to keep close to the sequence of words in the poems—Bonhoeffer clearly thought carefully about where he wanted to start and finish lines, where he wanted to break lines, and in poetry the form is also part of the meaning.

No translation is perfect, of course, but I hope that the accessibility and directness of Bonhoeffer's poetry, and his prose, inspires you to read more of his work, and be inspired by his life.

Notes on: About the translation

Bonhoeffer had learned to do when preaching in Berlin in the 1930s: Elizabeth Raum, *Dietrich Bonhoeffer: Called by God*, Continuum, London, 2003, p. 60.

With every power of good: Dietrich Bonhoeffer, edited by Eberhard Bethge, *Letters and Papers from Prison*, Schuster and Schuster, New York, 1992, p. 399.

By kindly, faithful, tranquil powers: Dietrich Bonhoeffer and Maria von Wedemeyer edited by Ruth Alice von Bismarck and Ulkrich Kabitz, John Brownjohn, tr., *Love Letters from Cell 92: The Correspondence between Dietrich Bonhoeffer and Maria von Wedemeyer 1943-1945*, Harper Collins, New York, 1994, p. 228.

By loving forces silently surrounded: Hilmar H. Werner, see CD recording, My Silent Wake / Pÿlon, Empyrean Rose, QLR-511311-2 2013 (Quam Libet, Switzerland, 2013), track 9.

Index

Lightning Source UK Ltd.
Milton Keynes UK
UKHW020745290120
357813UK00014B/1133

9 780647 530627